Performance Assessment

TEACHER'S GUIDE

- INTERVIEW/TASK TESTS

- QUARTERLY EXTENDED PERFORMANCE ASSESSMENTS
  SCORING RUBRICS
  SAMPLE STUDENT PAPERS
  PERFORMANCE INDICATORS
  ANSWER KEYS

- MANAGEMENT FORMS

Grade 1

Harcourt Brace & Company

rlando • Atlanta • Austin • Boston • San Francisco • Chicago • Dallas • New York • Toronto • London

http://www.hbschool.com

Printed in the United States of America

ISBN 0-15-311178-X

9 10 11 12 13 14 15 16 17 18 19 20 022 2006 2005 2004 2003 2002 2001

CONTENTS

▶ **Evaluating Interview/Task Test Items**

▶ **Interview Task/Test and Evaluation Criteria**

Performance Assessment Program

Unique Features of Math Advantage Performance Assessment

To create assessments that actually evaluate what is taught, it is necessary to target specific math concepts, skills, and strategies at each grade level. In planning the assessment program for *Math Advantage,* a review was made of performance assessments cited in professional literature and also of those used in state testing programs. Comparisons were made among available models and desirable features were identified. Holistic scoring was chosen as the primary method of scoring. The *Math Advantage* Performance assessments offer the following features:

- **They model good instruction**
  The assessments are like mini lessons.

- **They are diagnostic.**
  By reviewing students' notes, teachers gain valuable insight into the thinking strategies that students are using.

- **They encourage the thinking process.**
  The assessments guide students through the process of organizing their thoughts and revising their strategies as they solve problems.

- **They are flexible.**
  No strict time limits are imposed,and students are encourage to proceed at their own pace.

- **They use authentic instruction.**
  Each task is based on realistic problem-solving situations.

- **They are scored holistically.**
  Each student's responses are scored holistically to provide a comprehensive view of his or her performance.

Development of the Performance Assessment Program

Each assessment was field-tested with students before it was selected for inclusion in the program. After the assessments were selected, the pool of student papers for each assessment was reviewed and model papers were selected to illustrate the various scores. Annotations were then written for each model paper, explaining why the score was given.

The development process provided an opportunity to drop or correct those assessments that were not working as expected.

Administering the Performance Assessments

- **Be encouraging.**
  Your role in administering the assessments should be that of a coach, motivating, guiding, and encouraging students to produce their best work.

- **Be clear.**
  The directions for the assessments are not standardized. If necessary, you may rephrase them for students.

- **Be supportive.**
  You may assist students who need help. The amount of assistance needed will vary depending on the needs and abilities of your students.

- **Be fair.**
  Allow students adequate time to do their best work. They should not feel that they could have done better if they had been given enough time.

- **Be flexible.**
  All students need not proceed through the assessments at the same rate and in the same manner.

- **Be involving.**
  Whenever possible, involve students in the evaluation process.

Providing for Students with Special Needs

Many school districts are facing the challenge of adapting instruction and assessment to make them appropriate for their learners with special needs. Because the performance assessments are not standardized, the procedure for administering them can be adjusted to meet the needs of these learners. Teachers can help students who have difficulty responding by

- pairing a less proficient learner with a more proficient learner.

- encouraging students to discuss their ideas with a partner.

- providing an audiotape of the performance assessment and having students read along with the narration.

- permitting students to record tapes their response in lieu of a writing them.

- allowing students to do their initial planning, computing, designing, and drafting on the computer.

- giving students extra time to do their planning.

- providing assistance upon request.

Keep in mind, however, that the more the performance assessments are modified, the less reliable they may be as measures of students' mathematical ability.

Scoring Rubrics for Mathematics

In scoring a student's task, the teacher should ask two questions: *How well did the student use the conventions of mathematics to arrive at a solution?* and *How well did the student communicate the solution?* The scoring system used for the performance assessments is designed to be compatible with those used by many state assessment programs. Using a 4-point scale, the teacher classifies the student's performance as "excellent," "adequate," "limited," or "little or no achievement". A Score 3 paper shows evidence of extensive understanding of content and provides an exceptionally clear and effective solution. A Score 2 paper shows an acceptable understanding of content and provides a solution that shows reasonable insight. A Score 1 paper shows partial understanding and is clear in some parts, but not in others. A Score 0 paper demonstrates poor understanding of content and provides a solution that is unclear.

4-Point Scale			
Excellent Achievement	Adequate Achievement	Limited Achievement	Little or No Achievement
3	2	1	0

Sharing Results with Students and Parents

The performance assessment can provide valuable insights into students' mathematical abilities by revealing how all students performed on a common task. However, it is important that their performance on the assessment be interpreted in light of other samples that have been collected such as daily papers, student portfolios, and other types of tests, as well as teacher observation.

For Students

Discuss the rubric with students and explain how it is used. You may even want to score some anonymous papers as a group or have students score each other's papers and discuss the criteria as they apply to those papers. Make photocopies of the rubrics to use for individual reports. Discuss the reports in conferences with students, pointing out their strengths as well as areas in which they could still improve.

For Parents

Results of performance assessments may also be shared with parents, who will. appreciate seeing what their children can do. Show parents the performance assessment so that they understand the task that the students were asked to perform. Show their child's responses and discuss the strengths and weaknesses of the responses. Explain the scoring rubric and how the responses were evaluated. Show parents model papers that illustrate the range in student performance to help them put their child's paper in perspective.

Using Results to Assign Grades

No single test, whether a standardized achievement test, a performance assessment, or an open-ended test, can fully measure a student's mathematical ability. For this reason it is important to use multiple measures of assessment. Therefore, a score on performance assessment should not be used as the sole determiner of a report-card grade or semester grade. The performance assessment could represent one of several factors used to determine a student's grade. Assessments could be combined with the results of a selection of tests, daily grades, class participation, self-reflections, and various samples collected in a portfolio. The following table shows how holistic scores can be converted into numerical or letter grades.

Holistic Score	Letter Grade	Numerical Grade
3	A	90-100
2	B	80-89
1	C	70-79
0	D-F	60 or below

Developing Your Own Rubric

A well-written rubric can help teachers score students' work more accurately and fairly. It also gives students a better idea of what qualities their work should exhibit. Using performance assessment to make connections between teaching and learning requires both conceptual and reflective involvement. Determining criteria may be the most difficult aspect of the process of developing assessment criteria on which to evaluate students' performance. Particularly challenging is the task of finding the right language to describe the qualities of student performance that distinguishes mediocre and excellent work. Teachers should begin the process of developing rubrics by

- gathering sample rubrics as models to be adapted as needed.

- selecting samples of students' work that represent a range of quality.

- determining the qualities of work that distinguish good examples from poor examples.

- using those qualities to write descriptors for the desired characteristics.

- continually revising the criteria until the rubric score reflects the quality of work indicated.

Your Own **Scoring Rubric**

Response Level	Criteria
Score 3	**Generally accurate, complete, and clear** _____ _____ _____ _____
Score 2	**Partially accurate, complete, and clear** _____ _____ _____ _____
Score 1	**Minimally accurate, complete, and clear** _____ _____ _____ _____
Score 0	**Not accurate, complete, and clear** _____ _____ _____ _____

Math Advantage **Scoring Rubric**

Response Level	Criteria
Score 3	**Generally accurate, complete, and clear** _____ All or most parts of the task are successfully completed; the intents of all parts of the task are addressed with appropriate strategies and procedures. _____ There is evidence that the student has a clear understanding of key concepts and procedures. _____ Student work and explanations are clear. _____ Additional illustrations or information, if present, enhance communication. _____ Answers for all parts are correct or reasonable.
Score 2	**Partially accurate, complete, and clear** _____ Some parts of the task are successfully completed; other parts are attempted and their intents addressed, but they are not successfully completed. _____ There is evidence that the student has partial understanding of key concepts and procedures. _____ Some student work and explanations are clear, but it is necessary to make inferences to understand the response. _____ Additional illustrations or information, if present, may not enhance communication significantly. _____ Answers for some parts are correct, but partially correct or incorrect for others.
Score 1	**Minimally accurate, complete, and clear** _____ A part (or parts) of the task is (are) addressed with minimal success while other parts are omitted or incorrect. _____ There is minimal or limited evidence that the student understands concepts and procedures. _____ Student work and explanations may be difficult to follow, and it is necessary to fill in the gaps to understand the response. _____ Additional illustrations or information, if present, do not enhance communication and may be irrelevant. _____ Answers to most parts are incorrect.
Score 0	**Not accurate, complete, and clear** _____ No part of the task is completed with any success. _____ There is little, if any, evidence that the student understands key concepts and procedures. _____ Student work and explanations are very difficult to follow and may be incomprehensible. _____ Any additional illustrations, if present, do not enhance communication and are irrelevant. _____ Answers to all parts are incorrect.

PERFORMANCE ASSESSMENT

How Does Your Garden Grow?

Purpose
To assess student performance after completing Chapters 1–6

Time
10 to 15 minutes per task

Grouping
Individuals or partners

Overview
Explain to children that this performance assessment is about a vegetable garden. Each task is about things that could grow or be seen in a vegetable garden.

Task A-1   Spotting Bugs
Children are asked to draw spots on bugs and write the addends to show combinations that make 10.

Task A-2   Peas in a Pod
Children are asked to show subtraction situations, write how many are left, and draw a picture to show their work.

Task A-3   Tomato-Growing Contest!
Children are asked to read and interpret a chart, draw a picture, and use addition to solve problems.

Task A-4   What's the Scoop with Veggie Soup?
Children are asked to read and interpret a chart, fill in a table, and use comparative subtraction to solve problems.

How Does Your Garden Grow?

Task	Performance Indicators	Score (One score per task)
A-1	_____ draws a total of 10 spots on each bug _____ completes addition sentences for combinations that make 10	3 2 1 0
A-2	_____ subtracts correctly from 9 _____ draws pictures to show how many peas are left	3 2 1 0
A-3	_____ draws the correct number of tomatoes on each plant _____ adds to find out how many tomatoes each child grew _____ orders three single-digit numbers from greatest to least	3 2 1 0
A-4	_____ reads a recipe and fills in the correct numbers in a chart _____ finds the sums for doubles _____ subtracts to find how many are needed	3 2 1 0
	Total Score _____/12	

Teaching Plan
How Does Your Garden Grow?

Purpose

To assess the concepts, skills, and strategies that children have learned in Chapters 1–6

Start each task with some type of pre-assessment engagement activity. For example, read a story about a related topic. Children will benefit most from these tasks if they are completed individually. If you would like to group children, pairing is recommended. Have children talk about what they would do—for example, how they would draw a picture showing their work, using counting objects to illustrate. Then have each child do his or her work individually. After completing each assessment, follow up with a related post-assessment activity. For example, have children share their solutions with one another.

For most tasks, students are asked to show their work. Encourage children to show the pictures, words, or numerical expressions they use to arrive at their answers.

Task A-1 Spotting Bugs

Read the following to guide children through the task.

> Two bugs have 10 spots in all. Draw spots on these bugs. Write a math fact to show how many.

> Draw other pairs of bugs with 10 spots. Write a math fact for each pair.

Task A-2 Peas in a Pod

Read the following to guide children through the task.

> Pretend you have a pea pod like the one shown in the picture on your worksheet.

> How many peas are in this pod? Give 1 pea to a friend. Give 2 peas to another friend. How many peas are left for you? Draw a picture and show your work.

> You have another pea pod. Give 3 peas to one friend. Give 4 peas to another.

Task A-3 Tomato-Growing Contest!

Read the following to guide children through the task.

Sam, Tommy, and Janie enter a contest. Each child grows 2 tomato plants. Whoever grows the most tomatoes wins. Sam grows 4 tomatoes on one plant and 5 tomatoes on another. Tommy grows 2 tomatoes on one plant and 6 on another. Janie grows 5 tomatoes on one plant and 5 on another.

Draw the tomato plants. Who will win first place? second place? third place? How many tomatoes did each child grow?

Write addition facts to match your pictures.

Task A-4 What's the Scoop with Veggie Soup?

Read the following to guide children through the task.

Read the vegetable soup ingredients from the recipe card.

Your garden has
- 1 onion,
- 2 tomato plants with 2 tomatoes on each plant,
- 2 cornstalks with 3 ears of corn on each stalk, and
- 2 potato plants with 4 potatoes on each.

Does your garden have enough of each vegetable for the soup? Will you need to buy some from the store? Fill in the chart.

Add the total number of vegetables in the garden, and then subtract to find the number of vegetables that you need to buy.

12 Performance Assessment Chapters 1–6

How Does Your Garden Grow? A–1 to A–4

Spotting Bugs

Two bugs have 10 spots in all.
Draw spots on these bugs.
Write a math fact to show how many.

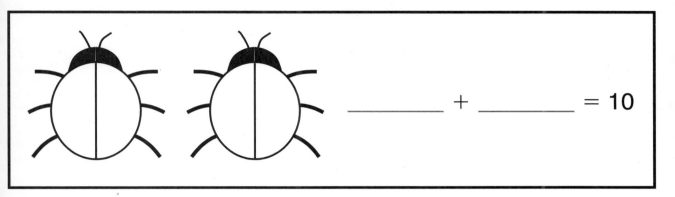

_____ + _____ = 10

Draw other pairs of bugs with 10 spots.
Write a math fact for each pair.

_____ + _____ = 10

_____ + _____ = 10

_____ + _____ = 10

_____ + _____ = 10

Peas in a Pod

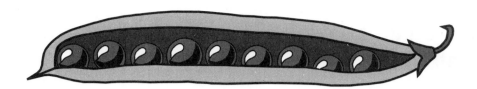

How many peas are in this pod? _____

Give 1 pea to a friend.
Give 2 peas to another friend.
How many peas are left for you? _____ peas

Draw a picture to show your work.

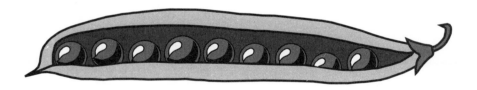

Here is another pea pod.
Give 3 peas to a friend.
Give 4 peas to another friend.
How many peas are left for you? _____ peas

Draw a picture and show your work.

Tomato-Growing Contest!

Sam, Tommy, and Janie enter a contest.
Each child grows 2 tomato plants.
Whoever grows the most tomatoes wins.

This chart shows
how many tomatoes
each child grew.

	Plant 1	**Plant 2**
Sam	4	5
Tommy	2	6
Janie	5	5

Draw the tomato plants.

Sam		**Tommy**		**Janie**	
Plant 1	Plant 2	Plant 1	Plant 2	Plant 1	Plant 2

Who will win? How many tomatoes?

1st place _____ _____

2nd place _____ _____

3rd place _____ _____

What's the Scoop with Veggie Soup?

Vegetable Soup	
3 cans of chicken broth	6 ears of corn
3 onions	9 potatoes
6 tomatoes	

Your garden has

1 .

2 🌿 with 2 🍅 on each.

2 🌿 with 3 🌽 on each.

2 🌿 with 4 🥔 on each.

Does your garden have enough of each vegetable for the soup? Will you need to buy some from the store? Fill in this chart.

	How Many for Soup?	How Many I Have?	How Many to Buy?
Onions			
Tomatoes			
Corn			
Potatoes			

CHAPTERS
1-6

Peas in a Pod

Name

How many peas are in this pod? 9

Give 1 pea to a friend.
Give 2 peas to another friend.
How many peas are left for you? 6 peas

Draw a picture to show your work.

Check children's drawings.
Drawing should show 6 peas.

Here is another pea pod.
Give 3 peas to a friend.
Give 4 peas to another friend.
How many peas are left for you? 2 peas

Draw a picture and show your work.

Check children's drawings.
Drawing should show 2 peas.

How Does Your Garden Grow? A–2

14

CHAPTERS
1-6

Spotting Bugs

Name

Two bugs have 10 spots in all.
Draw spots on these bugs.
Write a math fact to show how many.

$5 + 5 = 10$

Draw other pairs of bugs with 10 spots.
Write a math fact for each pair.

Possible Answers:
Order may be reversed.
Check children's drawings.

$6 + 4 = 10$

$9 + 1 = 10$

$2 + 8 = 10$

$3 + 7 = 10$

How Does Your Garden Grow? A–1

13

What's the Scoop with Veggie Soup?

CHAPTERS 1-6

Name _____

Vegetable Soup

3 cans of chicken broth	6 ears of corn
3 onions	9 potatoes
6 tomatoes	

Your garden has

1 _____ .

2 _____ with 2 _____ on each.

2 _____ with 3 _____ on each.

2 _____ with 4 _____ on each.

Does your garden have enough of each vegetable for the soup? Will you need to buy some from the store? Fill in this chart.

	How Many for Soup?	How Many I Have?	How Many to Buy?
Onions	3	1	2
Tomatoes	6	4	2
Corn	6	6	0
Potatoes	9	8	1

16

How Does Your Garden Grow? A–4

Tomato-Growing Contest!

CHAPTERS 1-6

Name _____

Sam, Tommy, and Janie enter a contest.
Each child grows 2 tomato plants.
Whoever grows the most tomatoes wins.

This chart shows how many tomatoes each child grew.

	Plant 1	Plant 2
Sam	4	5
Tommy	2	6
Janie	5	5

Draw the tomato plants.

Sam		Tommy		Janie	
Plant 1	Plant 2	Plant 1	Plant 2	Plant 1	Plant 2

Who will win? How many tomatoes?

1st place ___Janie___ 10

2nd place ___Sam___ 9

3rd place ___Tommy___ 8

15

How Does Your Garden Grow? A–3

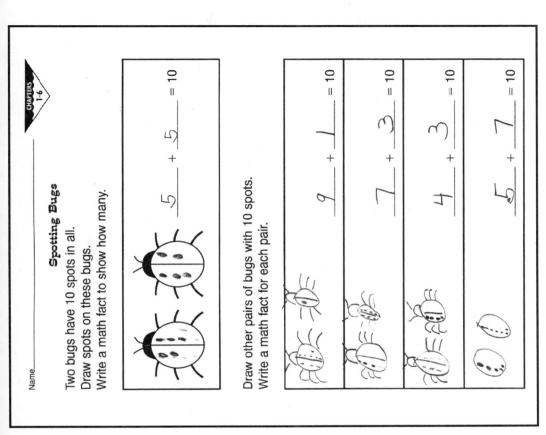

Spotting Bugs

Name _____

Two bugs have 10 spots in all.
Draw spots on these bugs.
Write a math fact to show how many.

$$5 + 5 = 10$$

Draw other pairs of bugs with 10 spots.
Write a math fact for each pair.

$$9 + 1 = 10$$

$$7 + 3 = 10$$

$$4 + 3 = 10$$

$$5 + 7 = 10$$

Level 2 The child has successfully completed some of the task. The diagrams are clear, but the sums are not always 10. The child has a partial understanding of addends to 10.

A–1

Spotting Bugs

Name _____

Two bugs have 10 spots in all.
Draw spots on these bugs.
Write a math fact to show how many.

$$0 + 10 = 10$$

Draw other pairs of bugs with 10 spots.
Write a math fact for each pair.

$$2 + 8 = 10$$

$$9 + 1 = 10$$

$$7 + 3 = 10$$

$$4 + 6 = 10$$

Level 3 The child has successfully completed all parts of this task. The child's diagrams clearly demonstrate an understanding of addends to 10.

How Does Your Garden Grow?

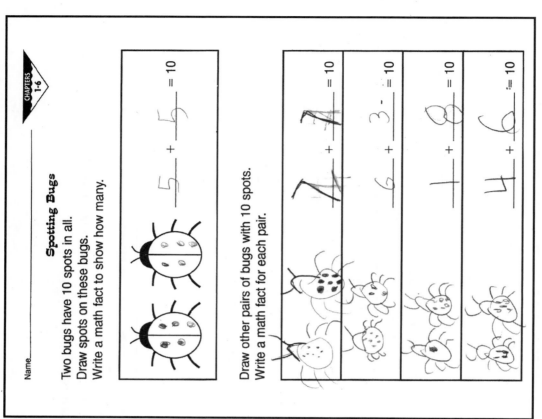

CHAPTERS 1-6

Name _____

Spotting Bugs

Two bugs have 10 spots in all.
Draw spots on these bugs.
Write a math fact to show how many.

$5 + 5 = 10$

Draw other pairs of bugs with 10 spots.
Write a math fact for each pair.

$7 + 7 = 10$

$6 + 3 - = 10$

$8 + = 10$

$4 + 6 := 10$

Level 1 The child has attempted the task. Most drawings are accurate, but the answers are incorrect. There is no evidence that the child understands addition.

TEACHER NOTES

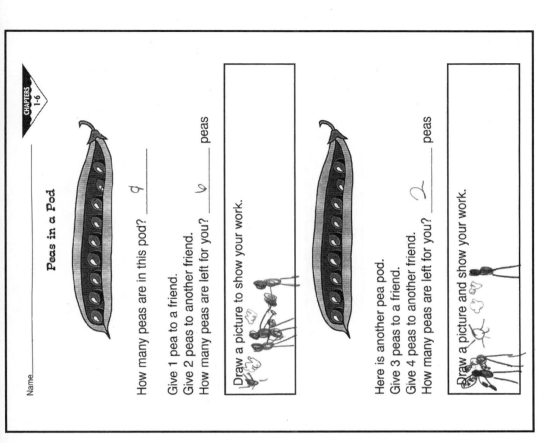

CHAPTERS 1-6

Name _____

Peas in a Pod

How many peas are in this pod? ____ q

Give 1 pea to a friend.
Give 2 peas to another friend.
How many peas are left for you? ____ 6 peas

Draw a picture to show your work.

Here is another pea pod.
Give 3 peas to a friend.
Give 4 peas to another friend.
How many peas are left for you? ____ 2 peas

Draw a picture and show your work.

Level 2 The child has successfully subtracted from 9, but the work is unclear. It is not clear what strategy was used. The child may or may not understand the concept.

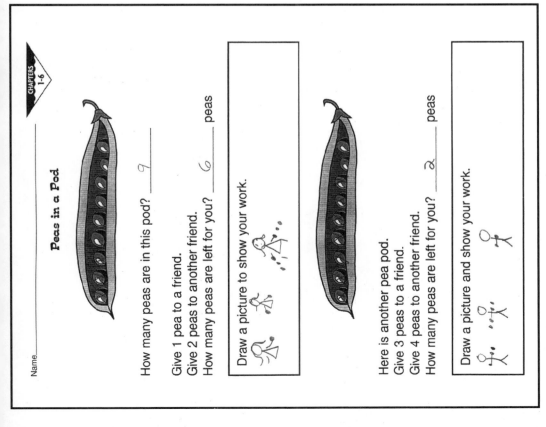

CHAPTERS 1-6

Name _____

Peas in a Pod

How many peas are in this pod? ____ q

Give 1 pea to a friend.
Give 2 peas to another friend.
How many peas are left for you? ____ 6 peas

Draw a picture to show your work.

Here is another pea pod.
Give 3 peas to a friend.
Give 4 peas to another friend.
How many peas are left for you? ____ 2 peas

Draw a picture and show your work.

Level 3 The child has successfully completed this task. The drawings are clear and accurate. The child has crossed off peas in the pods, which shows an understanding of the concept.

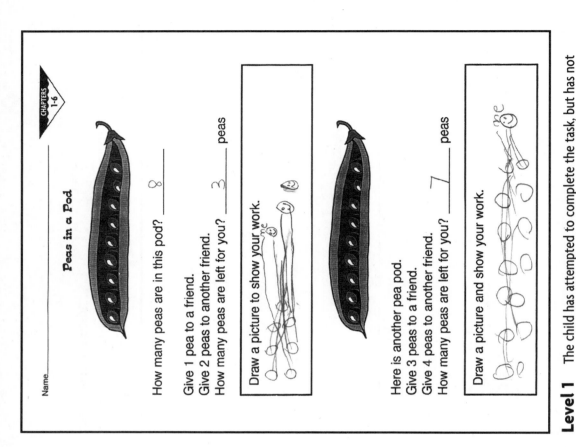

Peas in a Pod

Name_____

How many peas are in this pod? _____ 8

Give 1 pea to a friend.
Give 2 peas to another friend.
How many peas are left for you? _____ 3 _____ peas

Draw a picture to show your work.

Here is another pea pod.
Give 3 peas to a friend.
Give 4 peas to another friend.
How many peas are left for you? _____ 7 _____ peas

Draw a picture and show your work.

CHAPTERS
1-6

Level 1 The child has attempted to complete the task, but has not been successful. It is not clear what strategy is used. The child does not understand the concept.

TEACHER NOTES

Name _____

Tomato Growing Contest!

Sam, Tommy, and Janie enter a contest.
Each child grows 2 tomato plants.
Whoever grows the most tomatoes wins.

This chart shows
how many tomatoes
each child grew.

	Plant 1	Plant 2
Sam	4	5
Tommy	2	6
Janie	5	5

Draw the tomato plants.

Sam		Tommy		Janie	
Plant 1	Plant 2	Plant 1	Plant 2	Plant 1	Plant 2

Who will win? How many tomatoes?

1st place Janie   10

2nd place Sam   9

3rd place Tommy   8

Level 2 The child has answered completely and accurately, but the illustrations are incorrect. There is evidence that the child has partial understanding of the concept.

Name _____

Tomato Growing Contest!

Sam, Tommy, and Janie enter a contest.
Each child grows 2 tomato plants.
Whoever grows the most tomatoes wins.

This chart shows
how many tomatoes
each child grew.

	Plant 1	Plant 2
Sam	4	5
Tommy	2	6
Janie	5	5

Draw the tomato plants.

Sam		Tommy		Janie	
Plant 1	Plant 2	Plant 1	Plant 2	Plant 1	Plant 2

Who will win? How many tomatoes?

1st place Janie   10

2nd place Sam   9

3rd place Tommy   8

Level 3 The child has successfully completed the task. The illustrations demonstrate an understanding of addition. The child has correctly ordered the numbers.

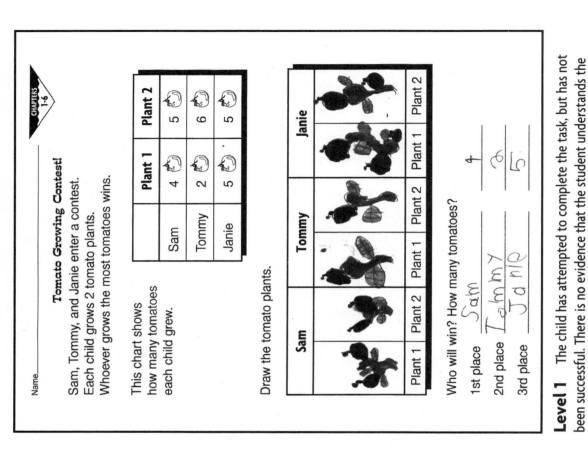

CHAPTERS
1-6

Name _____

Tomato Growing Contest!

Sam, Tommy, and Janie enter a contest.
Each child grows 2 tomato plants.
Whoever grows the most tomatoes wins.

This chart shows
how many tomatoes
each child grew.

	Plant 1	Plant 2
Sam	4	5
Tommy	2	6
Janie	5	5

Draw the tomato plants.

Sam		Tommy		Janie	
Plant 1	Plant 2	Plant 1	Plant 2	Plant 1	Plant 2

Who will win? How many tomatoes?

1st place   Sam   4

2nd place   Tommy   6

3rd place   Janie   5

Level 1   The child has attempted to complete the task, but has not been successful. There is no evidence that the student understands the concept. Answers are incorrect.

TEACHER NOTES

A-4

CHAPTERS
1-6

Name _____

What's the Scoop with Veggie Soup?

Vegetable Soup

3 cans of chicken broth	6 ears of corn
3 onions	9 potatoes
6 tomatoes	

Your garden has

1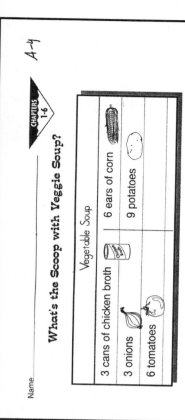

2 🌱🌱 with 2 🍅 on each.

2 with 3 🌽 on each.

2 with 4 🥔 on each.

Does your garden have enough of each vegetable for the soup? Will you need to buy some from the store? Fill in this chart.

	How Many for Soup?	How Many I Have?	How Many to Buy?
Onions	3	1	2
Tomatoes	6	2	4
Corn	0	3	3
Potatoes	1	4	1

Level 2 The child has successfully completed parts of the task. Some answers are correct, but others are not. The child demonstrates a partial understanding of the concept.

A-4

CHAPTERS
1-6

Name _____

What's the Scoop with Veggie Soup?

Vegetable Soup

3 cans of chicken broth	6 ears of corn
3 onions	9 potatoes
6 tomatoes	

Your garden has

1 🧅

2 🌱 with 2 🍅 on each. 4

2 with 3 🌽 on each. 6

2 with 4 🥔 on each. 8

Does your garden have enough of each vegetable for the soup? Will you need to buy some from the store? Fill in this chart.

	How Many for Soup?	How Many I Have?	How Many to Buy?
Onions	3	1	2
Tomatoes	6	4	2
Corn	6	6	0
Potatoes	9	8	0

Level 3 The child has successfully completed all parts of the task. The table is accurately filled in. There is evidence that the child understands comparative subtraction.

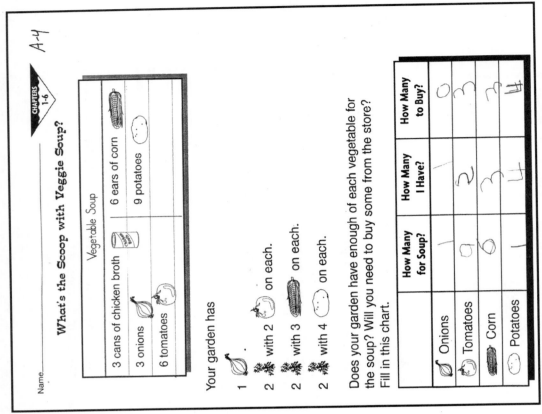

A-4

CHAPTERS
1-6

What's the Scoop with Veggie Soup?

Name _____

Vegetable Soup

3 cans of chicken broth	6 ears of corn
3 onions	9 potatoes
6 tomatoes	

Your garden has

1 🧅 .

2 🌿 with 2 on each.

2 🌽 with 3 on each.

2 ⚪ with 4 on each.

Does your garden have enough of each vegetable for the soup? Will you need to buy some from the store? Fill in this chart.

	How Many for Soup?	How Many I Have?	How Many to Buy?
🧅 Onions			0
🍅 Tomatoes	6	2	3
🌽 Corn		3	3
⚪ Potatoes			4

Level 1 The child has attempted all parts of the task. Answers to most parts are incorrect. There is limited evidence that the student understands the concept.

TEACHER NOTES

Baby Chicks

Purpose
To assess student performance after completing Chapters 7–15

Materials
crayons

Time
10 to 15 minutes per task

Grouping
Individuals or partners

Overview
Explain to children that this performance assessment is about baby chicks.

Task B-1   Hatching Eggs
Children are asked to use a number pattern to complete a chart and draw a picture to show the pattern.

Task B-2   Even and Odd Chicks
Children are asked to color pictures to show even and odd numbers, explain the pattern, and count by twos and tens.

Task B-3   Mystery Pen
Children are asked to draw a figure on a coordinate grid, identify the figure, and determine if the figure is open or closed.

Task B-4   All Penned Up!
Children are asked to draw figures with given numbers of sides and corners; draw pictures inside, outside, or on the figures; and subtract from 12.

Baby Chicks

Task	Performance Indicators	Score (One score per task)
B-1	_____ continues a number pattern _____ draws a picture that shows a doubles pattern	3 2 1 0
B-2	_____ colors even numbers yellow and odd numbers tan _____ explains the even and odd color pattern _____ circles groups of twos and tens and counts the groups	3 2 1 0
B-3	_____ draws a triangle in the correct place on a coordinate grid _____ identifies and writes the name of the figure drawn on the coordinate grid _____ identifies a triangle as a closed figure	3 2 1 0
B-4	_____ draws a figure with the correct number of sides _____ draws the correct number of chicks inside, outside, and on a figure _____ counts, adds, and subtracts to find how many chicks are inside and outside the figures	3 2 1 0
	Total Score _____/12	

Teaching Plan
Baby Chicks

Purpose
To assess the concepts, skills, and strategies that children have learned in Chapters 7–15

Materials
For each child crayons

Children will benefit most from these tasks if they are completed individually. If you would like to group children, pairing is recommended. Have children talk about what they would draw to illustrate what they do. Then have children draw their own pictures and show individually their thinking and strategies.

Task B-1 Hatching Eggs

Read the following to guide children through the task.

> Today is the big day. The eggs are about to hatch. The eggs hatch every hour. At 6:00 A.M., 1 egg hatches. At 7:00 A.M., 2 eggs hatch. At 8:00 A.M., 4 eggs hatch. Draw eggs in the table to complete the pattern.
>
> How many eggs will hatch at 9:00 A.M.? at 10:00 A.M.?
>
> Show how the eggs make a pattern.

Task B-2 Even and Odd Chicks

Tell children that they will be counting chicks in various ways. Have them look at the drawings of the chicks. They should notice that there is an equal number of chicks in each row. Read the following to guide children through the task.

> Color the even-numbered chicks yellow. Color the odd-numbered chicks tan.
>
> Tell about the pattern you see.
>
> Count the chicks by twos. Circle each group of 2. How many groups did you circle?
>
> Count the chicks by tens. Circle each group of 10. How many groups did you circle?

Task B-3 Mystery Pen

Explain to children that they are going to use a grid to make a picture of a pen for the chicks.

Then read the following to guide children through the task.

> Look at the table. It will tell you how many spaces *right* and *up* to move on the grid. For each move, start at the corner of the grid labeled with a star, move the correct number of spaces, and draw a dot on the grid. Connect the dots on the grid to make a pen for the chicks.
>
> What is the shape of the pen you made? Is it an open or closed shape?

Task B-4 All Penned Up!

Find a children's book about chicks that you can read aloud prior to this task. Review the terms *inside, outside,* and *on.* Then read the following to guide children through the task.

> You have 12 chicks. Draw a pen with 5 sides. Draw 1 chick <u>on</u> each side of the pen.
>
> Draw a pen with 4 sides. Draw 1 chick in each corner <u>inside</u> the pen.
>
> How many of the 12 chicks are left? Draw them <u>outside</u> of the pen.
>
> Find how many chicks are <u>inside</u> the pen.
> How many chicks are <u>outside</u> the pen?

Hatching Eggs

Today is the big day.
The eggs are about to hatch.
Fill in the eggs to
finish the pattern.

6:00 A.M.	1 egg hatches	◯
7:00 A.M.	2 eggs hatch	◯ ◯
8:00 A.M.	4 eggs hatch	◯ ◯ ◯ ◯
9:00 A.M.	_____ eggs hatch	
10:00 A.M.	_____ eggs hatch	

Show how the eggs make a pattern.

Name_____

Even and Odd Chicks

Color the even numbered chicks yellow.
Color the odd numbered chicks tan.

Tell about the pattern you see.

  Count the chicks by twos.
Circle each group of 2.
How many groups did you circle? _____

  Count the chicks by tens.
Circle each group of ten.
How many groups did you circle? _____

Mystery Pen

Moves	Right	Up
first	0	1
second	4	1
third	8	1
fourth	4	8

Make a pen for the chicks in the grid below. Connect the dots in order.

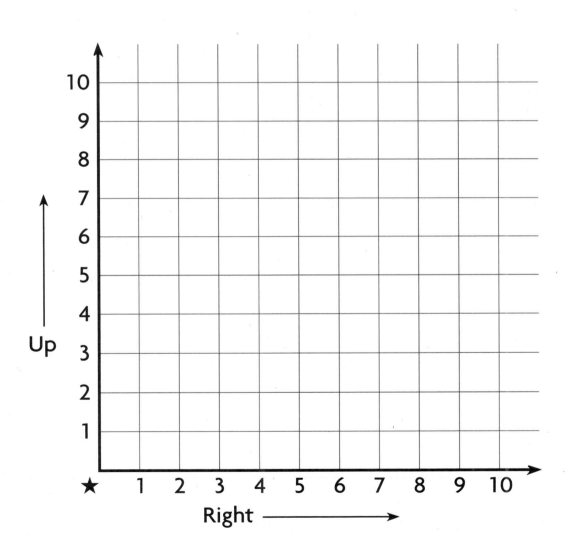

What shape is the pen formed by the dots? _____

Is it an open or closed shape? _____

All Penned Up!

You have 12 chicks.

Draw a pen with 5 sides. Draw 1 chick on each side.	Draw a pen with 4 sides. Draw 1 chick in each corner.

Draw the other chicks outside of the pens.

How many chicks are inside the pens? _____ chicks

How many chicks are outside the pens? _____ chicks

Baby Chicks B-4

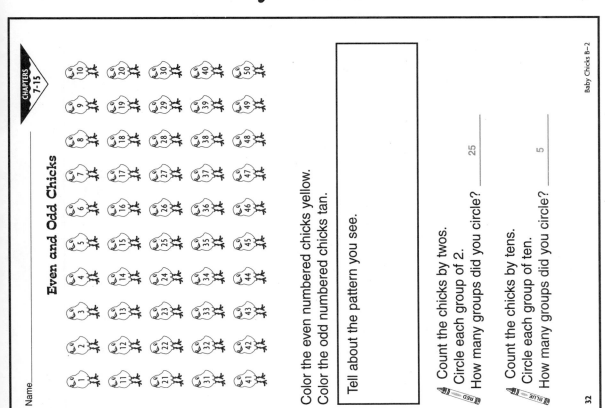

Even and Odd Chicks

Name _____

CHAPTERS
7-15

Color the even numbered chicks yellow.
Color the odd numbered chicks tan.

Tell about the pattern you see.

Count the chicks by twos.
Circle each group of 2.
How many groups did you circle? __25__

RED

Count the chicks by tens.
Circle each group of ten.
How many groups did you circle? __5__

BLUE

32

Baby Chicks B-2

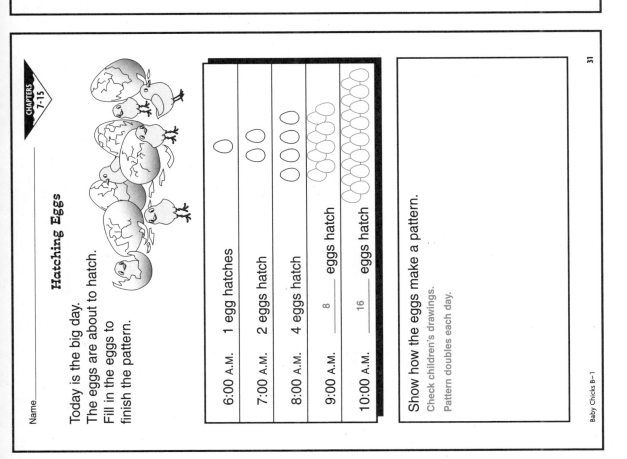

Hatching Eggs

Name _____

CHAPTERS
7-15

Today is the big day.
The eggs are about to hatch.
Fill in the eggs to
finish the pattern.

6:00 A.M.   1 egg hatches

7:00 A.M.   2 eggs hatch

8:00 A.M.   4 eggs hatch

9:00 A.M.   __8__ eggs hatch

10:00 A.M.   __16__ eggs hatch

Show how the eggs make a pattern.

Check children's drawings.
Pattern doubles each day.

31

Baby Chicks B-1

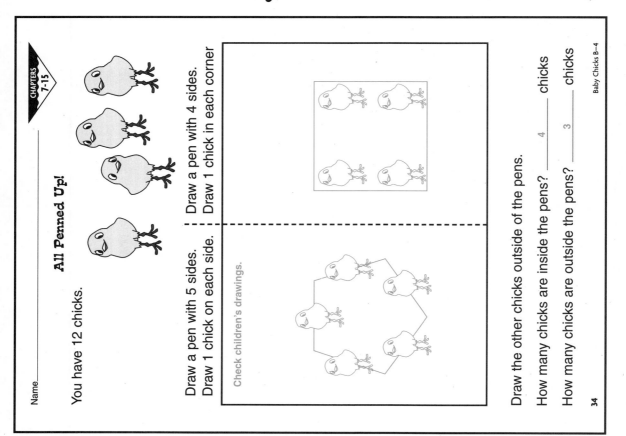

Name _____

All Penned Up!

You have 12 chicks.

Draw a pen with 5 sides.
Draw 1 chick on each side.

Check children's drawings.

Draw a pen with 4 sides.
Draw 1 chick in each corner.

Draw the other chicks outside of the pens.

How many chicks are inside the pens? ____4____ chicks

How many chicks are outside the pens? ____3____ chicks

Baby Chicks B-4

34

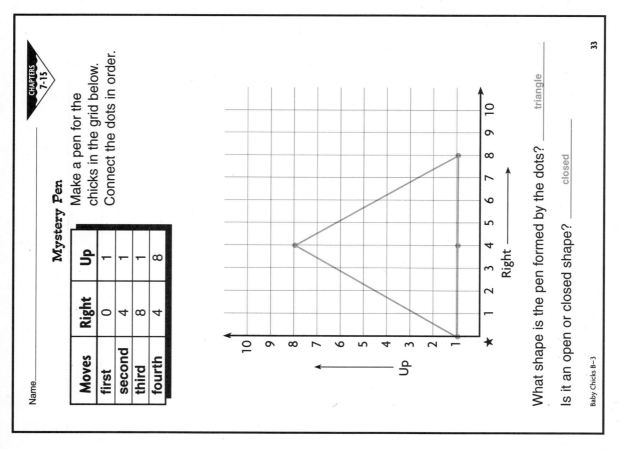

Name _____

Mystery Pen

Make a pen for the chicks in the grid below.
Connect the dots in order.

Moves	Right	Up
first	0	1
second	4	1
third	8	1
fourth	4	8

Up ←

Right →

What shape is the pen formed by the dots? _____triangle_____

Is it an open or closed shape? _____closed_____

Baby Chicks B-3

33

Model Student Papers for
Baby Chicks

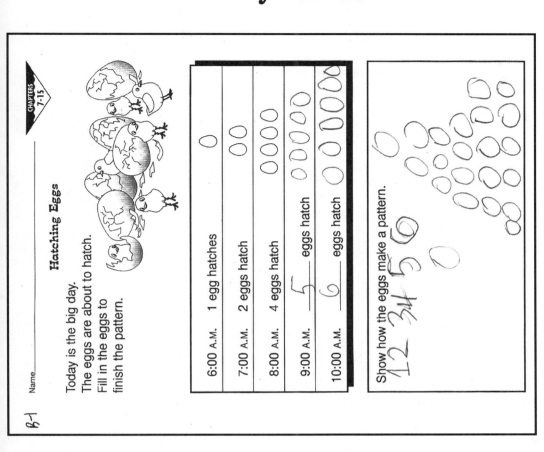

B-1

Hatching Eggs

Name _____

Today is the big day.
The eggs are about to hatch.
Fill in the eggs to finish the pattern.

6:00 A.M.	1 egg hatches	O
7:00 A.M.	2 eggs hatch	OO
8:00 A.M.	4 eggs hatch	OOOO
9:00 A.M.	__8__ eggs hatch	OOOOOOOO
10:00 A.M.	__16__ eggs hatch	OOOOOOOOOOOOOOOO

Show how the eggs make a pattern. It ow ees
adds on the same nober thet
it is

Level 3 The child has successfully completed all parts of the task. The work and explanations are clear and show that the child has an understanding of the concept of doubles.

B-1

Hatching Eggs

Name _____

Today is the big day.
The eggs are about to hatch.
Fill in the eggs to finish the pattern.

6:00 A.M.	1 egg hatches	O
7:00 A.M.	2 eggs hatch	OO
8:00 A.M.	4 eggs hatch	OOOO
9:00 A.M.	__5__ eggs hatch	OOOOO
10:00 A.M.	__6__ eggs hatch	OOOOOO

Show how the eggs make a pattern.
1 2 3 4 5 6

Level 2 The child has attempted all of the task and successfully completed some parts. There is evidence that the child understands the concept of patterns, but not of doubles.

Model Student Papers for
Baby Chicks

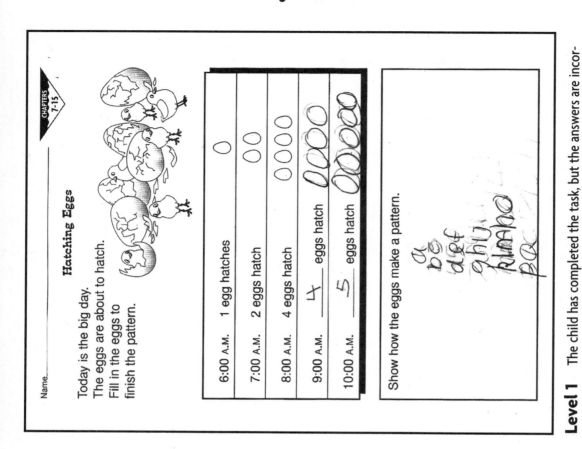

Hatching Eggs

Name

Today is the big day.
The eggs are about to hatch.
Fill in the eggs to finish the pattern.

6:00 A.M.   1 egg hatches

7:00 A.M.   2 eggs hatch

8:00 A.M.   4 eggs hatch

9:00 A.M.   4 ____ eggs hatch

10:00 A.M.   5 ____ eggs hatch

Show how the eggs make a pattern.

Level 1 The child has completed the task, but the answers are incorrect. There is no evidence that the child understands the concepts presented.

TEACHER NOTES

Model Student Papers for
Baby Chicks

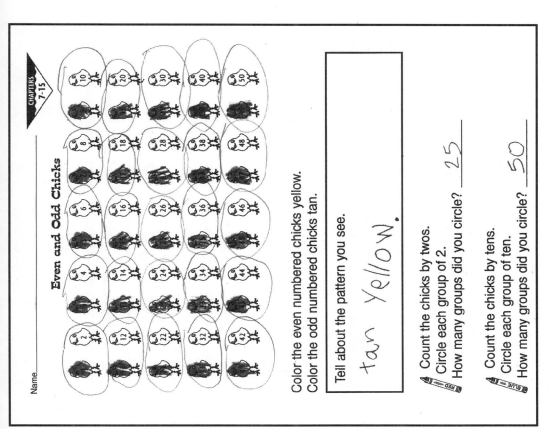

Name _____

Even and Odd Chicks

CHAPTERS 7-15

Color the even numbered chicks yellow.
Color the odd numbered chicks tan.

Tell about the pattern you see.

tan Yellow.

Count the chicks by twos.
Circle each group of 2.
How many groups did you circle? __25__

Count the chicks by tens.
Circle each group of ten.
How many groups did you circle? __50__

Level 2 The child has successfully completed parts of the task. There is evidence that the child understands odd and even and counting by twos, but not counting by tens.

Name _____

Even and Odd Chicks

CHAPTERS 7-15

Color the even numbered chicks yellow.
Color the odd numbered chicks tan.

Tell about the pattern you see. Every other

chick is Yellow.

Count the chicks by twos.
Circle each group of 2.
How many groups did you circle? __25__

Count the chicks by tens.
Circle each group of ten.
How many groups did you circle? __5__

Level 3 The child has succesfully completed all parts of the task. There is evidence that the child understands odd and even, counting by tens, and counting by twos.

Model Student Papers for
Baby Chicks

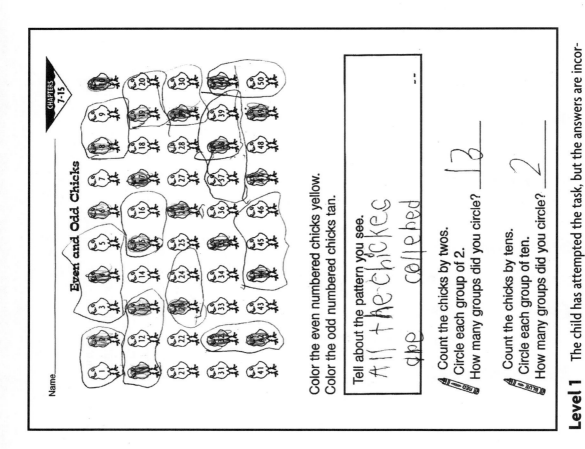

Name _____

Even and Odd Chicks

CHAPTERS 7-15

Color the even numbered chicks yellow.
Color the odd numbered chicks tan.

Tell about the pattern you see.

All the chickes are colleed

Count the chicks by twos.
Circle each group of 2.
How many groups did you circle? __13__

Count the chicks by tens.
Circle each group of ten.
How many groups did you circle? __2__

Level 1 The child has attempted the task, but the answers are incorrect. There is no evidence that the student understands the concepts presented.

TEACHER NOTES

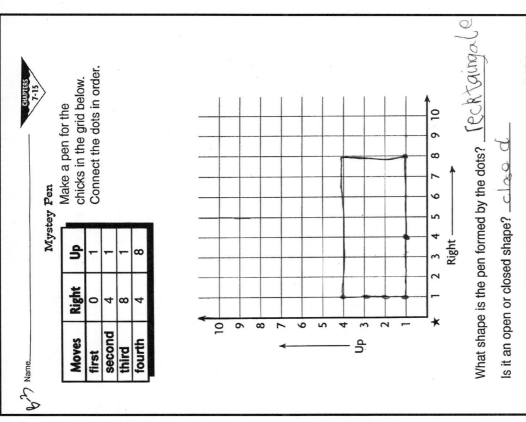

Left paper

Name

Mystey Pen

CHAPTERS 7-15

Make a pen for the chicks in the grid below. Connect the dots in order.

Moves	Right	Up
first	0	1
second	4	1
third	8	1
fourth	4	8

What shape is the pen formed by the dots? triangel

Is it an open or closed shape? closed

Level 3   The child has successfully completed all parts of the task. All answers are correct. There is evidence that the child understands the concepts presented.

Right paper

Name

Mystey Pen

CHAPTERS 7-15

Make a pen for the chicks in the grid below. Connect the dots in order.

Moves	Right	Up
first	0	1
second	4	1
third	8	1
fourth	4	8

What shape is the pen formed by the dots? rectaingale

Is it an open or closed shape? closed

Level 2   The child has successfully completed some of the task. There is evidence that the child understands open and closed shapes but not plotting points on a coordinate grid.

Model Student Papers for
Baby Chicks

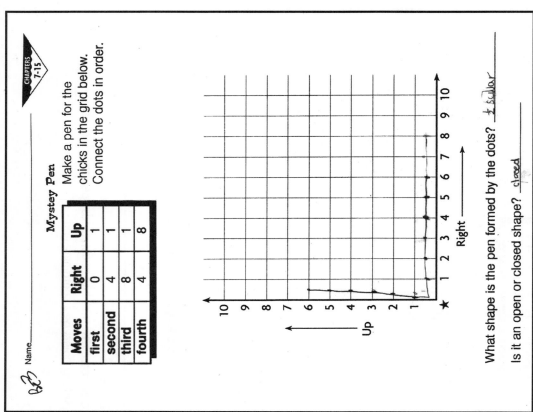

Name_____

Mystey Pen

CHAPTERS
7-15

Make a pen for the chicks in the grid below.
Connect the dots in order.

Moves	Right	Up
first	0	1
second	4	1
third	8	1
fourth	4	8

What shape is the pen formed by the dots? ↓ dollar

Is it an open or closed shape? closed

Level 1 The child has attempted all parts of the task, but the answers are incorrect. There is no evidence that the child understands open and closed shapes or coordinate grids.

TEACHER NOTES

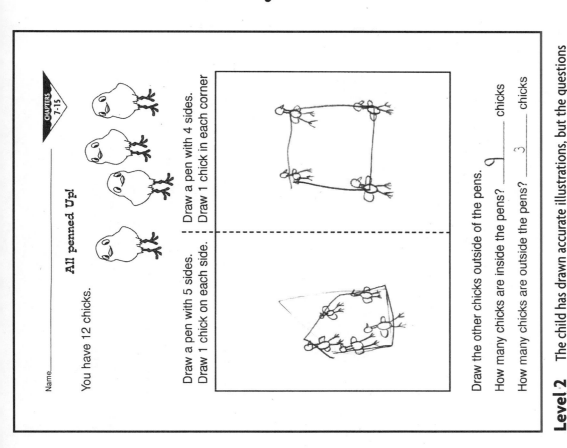

Level 2

CHAPTERS 7-15

All penned Up!

Name _____

You have 12 chicks.

Draw a pen with 5 sides.
Draw 1 chick on each side.

Draw a pen with 4 sides.
Draw 1 chick in each corner

Draw the other chicks outside of the pens.

How many chicks are inside the pens? __9__ chicks

How many chicks are outside the pens? __3__ chicks

Level 2 The child has drawn accurate illustrations, but the questions are answered incorrectly. There is limited evidence that the child understands the concepts of inside and outside.

Level 3

CHAPTERS 7-15

All penned Up!

Name _____

You have 12 chicks.

Draw a pen with 5 sides.
Draw 1 chick on each side.

Draw a pen with 4 sides.
Draw 1 chick in each corner

Draw the other chicks outside of the pens.

How many chicks are inside the pens? __4__ chicks

How many chicks are outside the pens? __3__ chicks

Level 3 The child has successfully completed all parts of the task. All answers are correct. The illustrations clearly demonstrate an understanding of *inside, outside,* and *on.*

Model Student Papers for
Baby Chicks

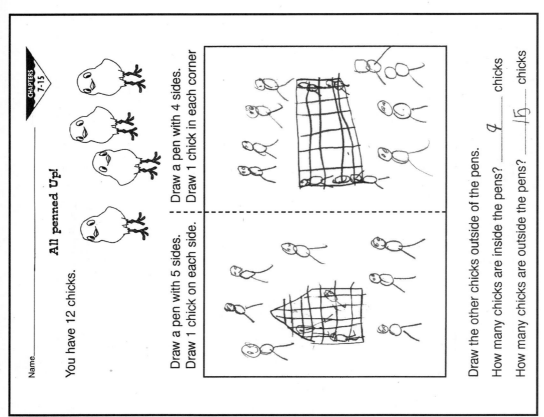

Name _____

All penned Up!

You have 12 chicks.

Draw a pen with 5 sides.
Draw 1 chick on each side.

Draw a pen with 4 sides.
Draw 1 chick in each corner.

Draw the other chicks outside of the pens.

How many chicks are inside the pens? ____ 9 ____ chicks

How many chicks are outside the pens? ____ 15 ____ chicks

Level 1   The child has attempted all parts of the task. The illustrations are clear, but there is no evidence that the child understands the concepts of inside and outside.

TEACHER NOTES

Chores

Purpose
To assess student performance after completing Chapters 16–24

Materials
real or punch-out coins, centimeter rulers

Time
10 to 15 minutes per task

Grouping
Individuals or partners

Overview
Explain to children that this performance assessment is about chores or tasks that children can do at home.

Task C-1   Friday Is Payday!
Children are asked to use a pattern to complete a chart, count dimes and pennies to find the total amount, and explain their answers.

Task C-2   Watch Me Grow!
Children are asked to use a ruler to measure height, use a pattern to make a prediction, and explain their answers.

Task C-3   Share Those Chores!
Children are asked to find a fraction of a group, draw a picture to show the fraction, and draw a different way to show the same fraction.

Task C-4   More Chores
Children are asked to count tally marks, make a bar graph, and answer questions about the graph.

Chores

Task	Performance Indicators	Score (One score per task)			
C-1	_____ continues a pattern _____ counts a collection of dimes and pennies _____ explains the pattern and how the coins were counted	3	2	1	0
C-2	_____ uses a centimeter ruler to measure height _____ makes a reasonable prediction _____ explains how the prediction was made	3	2	1	0
C-3	_____ draws a picture to show one half of 8, 6, 4, and 2 _____ draws a different way to show one half of the group	3	2	1	0
C-4	_____ counts tally marks and writes the total _____ makes a graph, including the title and labels _____ correctly answers questions about the graph	3	2	1	0

Total Score _____/12

Teaching Plan
Chores

Purpose
To assess the concepts, skills, and strategies that children have learned in chapters 16–24

Task C-1 Friday Is Payday!

Materials
For each child   real or punch-out coins if needed

Read the following to guide children through the task.

> Today you are going to pretend that. . .
> - on Sunday you get a penny for feeding the dog.
> - on Monday you get a dime for folding the clothes.
> - on Tuesday you get a penny for bringing in the mail.
> - on Wednesday you get a dime for sorting things to be recycled.
>
> Finish the pattern on the chart. How much money will you earn on Friday? Tell how you got your answer.
>
> How much money will you earn for the week? Show how you got your answer.

Task C-2 Watch Me Grow!

Materials
For each child   centimeter ruler

Read the following to guide children through the task.

> Your neighbor is growing plants from seeds to start a garden. You are helping by watering the seedlings each day after school. You use the centimeter ruler to measure one seedling to see how much it is growing.
>
> How tall is the seedling on the first day you measure it (day 1)?
> How much did the seedling grow after 5 days? Show how you know.
> How much did the seedling grow after 10 days? Show how you know.
> How tall do you think the seedling will be in 15 days? Tell how you know.

Task C-3 Share Those Chores!

Read the following to guide children through the task.

> You and your sister have chores to do.
> You and your sister need to
>   - wash 8 dishes.
>   - water 6 plants.
>   - empty 4 wastebaskets.
>   - make 2 beds.
>
> How will you share the chores so that each of you is doing one-half of the work? Draw a picture to show what you would do.
>
> Can you share the chores another way? One half of the work still needs to be done by each of you. Draw a picture to show another way.

Task C-4 More Chores

Read the following to guide children through the task.

> Some children took a survey. They asked 10 children to choose a "favorite chore." They made a tally table.
>
> Make a graph from the table. Title and label your graph. Now look at your graph. Which chore did the most children like best? Tell how you know.
>
> Compare "Cleaning My Bedroom" with "Feeding the Dog." How many more children picked "Feeding the Dog"? Show how you know.

Friday Is Pay Day!

Day	Chore	Money Earned
Sunday	🐕	1¢
Monday	👕	10¢
Tuesday	📬	1¢
Wednesday	♻	10¢
Thursday	🗑	
Friday	🧹	
Saturday	🌼	

Finish the pattern on the chart.
How much money will you earn on Friday? _____

Tell how you got your answer.

How much money will you earn for the

whole week? _____¢

Show how you got your answer.

Watch Me Grow!

1 day   **5 days**   **10 days**

How much did the seedling grow in 5 days? _____ cm

How much did the seedling grow in 10 days? _____ cm

How tall do you think the seedling will be in

15 days? _____ cm

Tell how you know.

Share Those Chores!

You and your sister have to do chores.

You and your sister need to
wash 8 dishes,

water 6 plants,

empty 4 wastebaskets,

and make 2 beds.

How will you share the chores so that each of

you is doing $\frac{1}{2}$ of the work?

Draw a picture to show what you and your sister would do.

Can you share the chores another way?

Draw a picture to show another way.

More Chores

Some children took a survey.
They asked 10 children to choose
a favorite chore.
They made a tally table.

Favorite Chores		Total
Taking out the Trash	|||	
Feeding the Dog	⊬⊬		
Cleaning My Bedroom			

Make a graph from
the table.
Title and label
your graph.

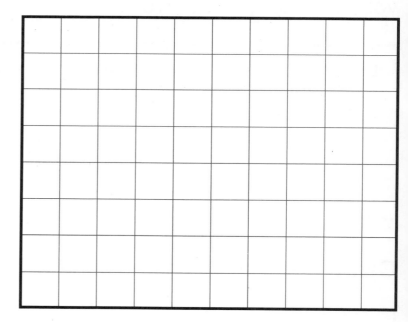

Look at your graph.
What is the favorite chore? _____

Compare "Cleaning My Bedroom" with "Feeding the Dog."

How many more children picked "Feeding the Dog"? _____

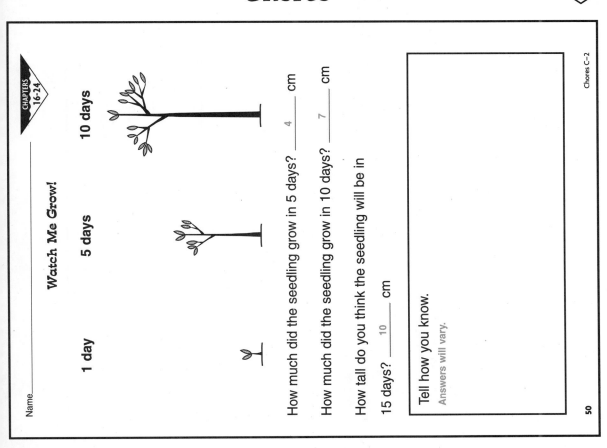

CHAPTERS
16-24

Name _____

Watch Me Grow!

| 1 day | 5 days | 10 days |

How much did the seedling grow in 5 days? _____4_____ cm

How much did the seedling grow in 10 days? _____7_____ cm

How tall do you think the seedling will be in

15 days? _____10_____ cm

Tell how you know.
Answers will vary.

Chores C–2

50

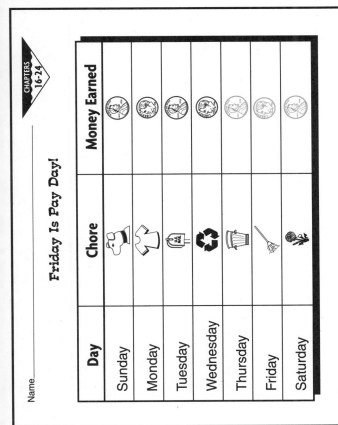

CHAPTERS
16-24

Name _____

Friday Is Pay Day!

Day	Chore	Money Earned
Sunday		
Monday		
Tuesday		
Wednesday		
Thursday		
Friday		
Saturday		

Finish the pattern on the chart.
How much money will you earn on Friday? _____ a dime

Tell how you got your answer.
Answers will vary.

How much money will you earn for the

whole week? _____34_____ ¢

Show how you got your answer.
Answers will vary.

Chores C–1

49

Name _____

More Chores

Some children took a survey.
They asked 10 children to choose
a favorite chore.
They made a tally table.

Favorite Chores		Total
Taking out the Trash	|||	3
Feeding the Dog	|||||		6
Cleaning My Bedroom			1

Make a graph from
the table.
Title and label
your graph.

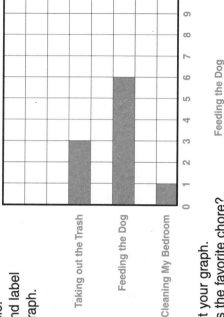

Taking out the Trash

Feeding the Dog

Cleaning My Bedroom

0 1 2 3 4 5 6 7 8 9

Feeding the Dog

Look at your graph.
What is the favorite chore? _____

Compare "Cleaning My Bedroom" with "Feeding the Dog."

How many more children picked "Feeding the Dog"? 5

Chores C–4

52

Name _____

Share Those Chores!

You and your sister have to do chores.

You and your sister need to

wash 8 dishes,

water 6 plants,

empty 4 wastebaskets,

and make 2 beds.

How will you share the chores so that each of
you is doing $\frac{1}{2}$ of the work?

Draw a picture to show what you and your sister would do.

Answers will vary.
Possible Answer:

Me

Sis

Can you share the chores another way?

Draw a picture to show another way.

Answers will vary.

Me

Sis

Chores C–3

51

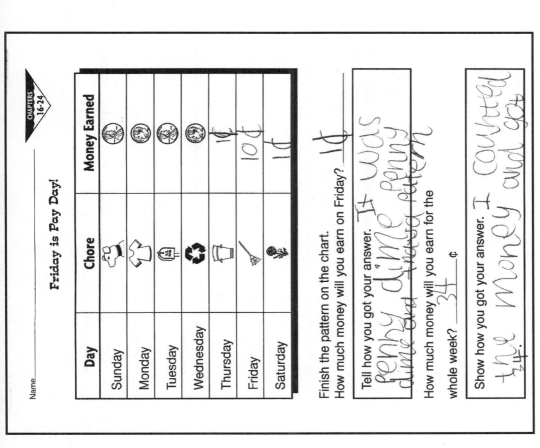

Paper 1 (Level 3)

Name _____

Friday is Pay Day!

CHAPTERS 16-24

Day	Chore	Money Earned
Sunday		1¢
Monday		10¢
Tuesday		1¢
Wednesday		10¢
Thursday	Penny	1¢
Friday	Dime	10¢
Saturday	Penny	1¢

Finish the pattern on the chart.
How much money will you earn on Friday? penny

Tell how you got your answer.
I Follod the Pattearn.

How much money will you earn for the
whole week? 34 ¢

Show how you got your answer.
1¢ 10¢ 10¢ 1¢ 1¢ 1¢ 1¢   34 ¢

Level 3 The child has successfully completed all parts of this task. The chart and answers demonstrate an understanding of using a pattern and counting coins.

Paper 2 (Level 2)

Name _____

Friday is Pay Day!

CHAPTERS 16-24

Day	Chore	Money Earned
Sunday		
Monday		
Tuesday		
Wednesday		
Thursday		1¢
Friday		10¢
Saturday		1¢

Finish the pattern on the chart.
How much money will you earn on Friday? 1¢

Tell how you got your answer.
penny dime penny dime and theird pattern

How much money will you earn for the
whole week? 34 ¢

Show how you got your answer. I counted the money and got 34¢.

Level 2 The child has successfully completed some of the task. The answer is correct but the pattern of coins on the chart is not drawn accurately.

Chores C–1

Performance Assessment Chapters 16–24 **55**

TEACHER NOTES

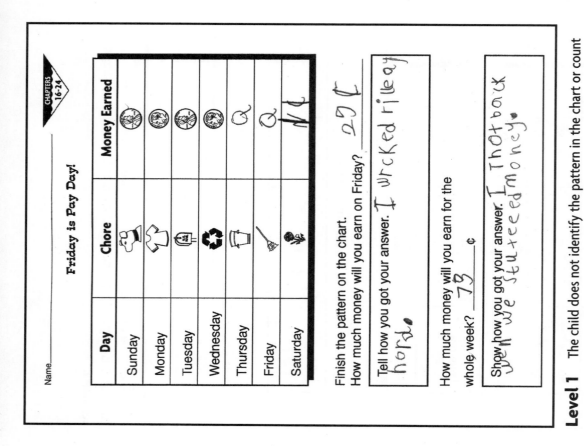

Friday is Pay Day!

Name _____

Day	Chore	Money Earned
Sunday		
Monday		
Tuesday		
Wednesday		
Thursday		
Friday		
Saturday		

Finish the pattern on the chart.
How much money will you earn on Friday? _____ 2 9 ¢

Tell how you got your answer. I wrcked rilleay hord.

How much money will you earn for the
whole week? _____ 73 _____ ¢

Show how you got your answer. I Thot bark we stu+eeed money.

Level 1 The child does not identify the pattern in the chart or count the coins correctly. The child does not understand the concept.

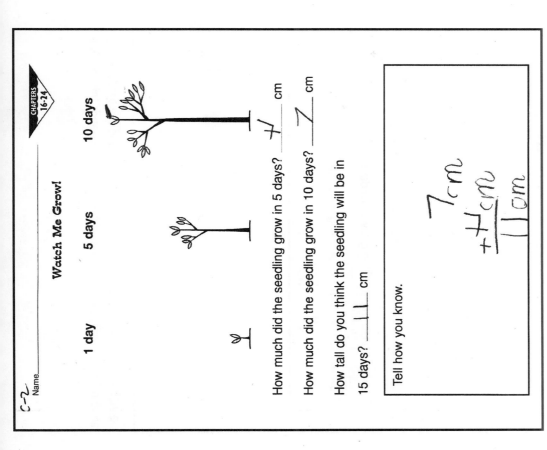

Level 2 The child has successfully measured and recorded the growth of the seedlings. The strategy of adding the growth of days 5 and 10 does not lead to an accurate prediction.

Level 3 The child has completed all parts of the task successfully. The child has used a centimeter ruler to measure the seedlings and then has made a reasonable prediction.

Chores

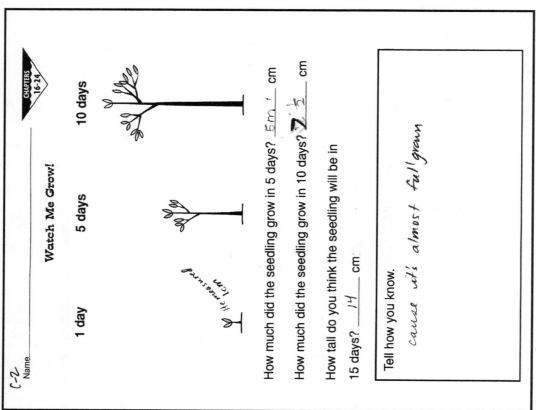

C-2
Name _____

CHAPTERS 16-24

Watch Me Grow!

1 day   5 days   10 days

He measured 1cm

How much did the seedling grow in 5 days? _5m 1_ cm

How much did the seedling grow in 10 days? _7.5_ cm

How tall do you think the seedling will be in

15 days? _14_ cm

Tell how you know.

cause it's almost full grown

TEACHER NOTES

Level 1 The child's measurements are inaccurate and the prediction is random. There is minimal evidence that the child understands the concept.

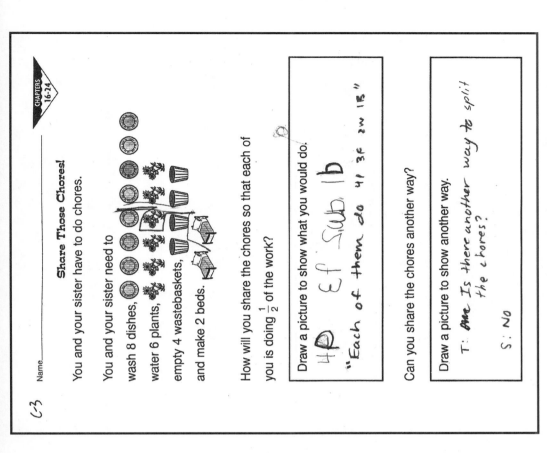

Level 2

Name _____ C-3

CHAPTERS
16-24

Share Those Chores!

You and your sister have to do chores.

You and your sister need to

wash 8 dishes,

water 6 plants,

empty 4 wastebaskets,

and make 2 beds.

How will you share the chores so that each of you is doing $\frac{1}{2}$ of the work?

Draw a picture to show what you would do.

4D Ef Sub 1b
"Each of them do 4l 3f 2w 1B"

Can you share the chores another way?

Draw a picture to show another way.

T: One Is there another way to split the chores?

S: No

Level 2 The child has successfully shown one half of a number, but has been unable to show another way to solve the problem. The child has some understanding of the concept.

Level 3

Name _____ C-3

CHAPTERS
16-24

Share Those Chores!

You and your sister have to do chores.

You and your sister need to

wash 8 dishes,

water 6 plants,

empty 4 wastebaskets,

and make 2 beds.

How will you share the chores so that each of you is doing $\frac{1}{2}$ of the work?

Draw a picture to show what you would do. I do 4 dishes, my sister does. 4 I do 3 plants, my sister does 3 flowers.

Can you share the chores another way?

Draw a picture to show another way. I do 2 wastebasket, my sister does 2. I do 1 bed, and my sister does one bed.

Chores C-3

Level 3 The child has completed all parts of the task successfully. The child's drawings clearly show one half of a number, which demonstrates an understanding of the concept.

Model Student Papers for
Chores

C-3 Name _____

Share Those Chores!

You and your sister have to do chores.

You and your sister need to

wash 8 dishes,

water 6 plants,

empty 4 wastebaskets,

and make 2 beds.

How will you share the chores so that each of you is doing $\frac{1}{2}$ of the work?

Draw a picture to show what you would do.

Can you share the chores another way?

Draw a picture to show another way.

Chores C-3

TEACHER NOTES

Level 1   The child has attempted to complete the task but has been unsuccessful. The drawings are not clear. The child does not understand the concept.

Model Student Papers for
Chores

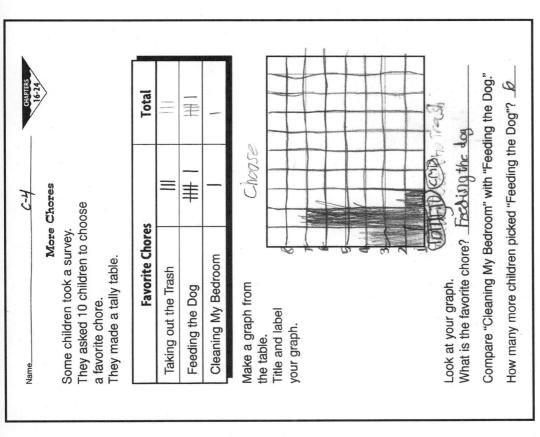

Top paper:

Name _____ C-4

More Chores

Some children took a survey.
They asked 10 children to choose
a favorite chore.
They made a tally table.

Favorite Chores		Total
Taking out the Trash	III	II
Feeding the Dog	₩I	₩I
Cleaning My Bedroom	I	I

Make a graph from
the table.
Title and label
your graph.

Choose

Look at your graph.
What is the favorite chore? _Feeding the dog_

Compare "Cleaning My Bedroom" with "Feeding the Dog."

How many more children picked "Feeding the Dog"? _6_

Level 2 The child successfully completed some parts of the task. The graph was labeled correctly but the tallies for one set of data were recorded incorrectly. The child may not understand the concept.

Bottom paper:

Name _____

More Chores

Some children took a survey.
They asked 10 children to choose
a favorite chore.
They made a tally table.

Favorite Chores		Total
Taking out the Trash	III	3
Feeding the Dog	₩I	6
Cleaning My Bedroom	I	I

Make a graph from _Favorite chores_
the table.
Title and label
your graph.

taking out the trash
feeding the dog
cleaning My Bedroom

Look at your graph.
What is the favorite chore? _Feeding the dog_

Compare "Cleaning My Bedroom" with "Feeding the Dog."

How many more children picked "Feeding the Dog"? _5_

Level 3 The child successfully completed all parts of the task. The child's tallies and graph clearly demonstrate an understanding of the concept of making a graph.

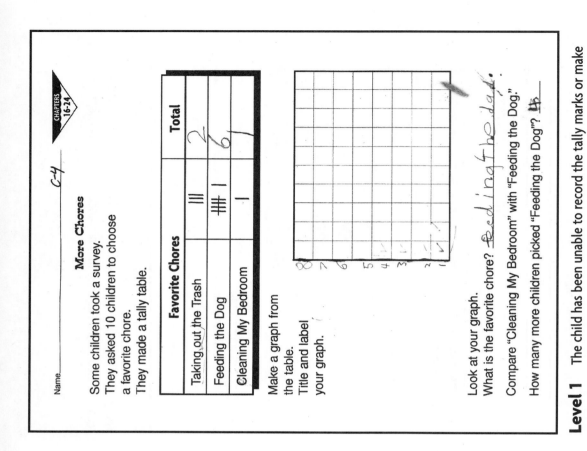

CHAPTERS
16-24

Name _____ C-4

More Chores

Some children took a survey.
They asked 10 children to choose
a favorite chore.
They made a tally table.

Favorite Chores		Total
Taking out the Trash	|||	2
Feeding the Dog	|||||	
Cleaning My Bedroom			6

Make a graph from
the table.
Title and label
your graph.

Look at your graph.
What is the favorite chore? _Feeding the dog._

Compare "Cleaning My Bedroom" with "Feeding the Dog."

How many more children picked "Feeding the Dog"? _4_

Level 1 The child has been unable to record the tally marks or make
the graph. The child does not understand the concept.

TEACHER NOTES

Pet Store

Purpose
To assess student performance after completing Chapters 25–28

Time
10 to 15 minutes per task

Grouping
Individuals or partners

Overview
Explain to children that this performance assessment is about a pet store.

Task D-1   Lots of Fish!
Children are asked to show two ways that 12 fish can be placed in two aquariums with an equal number of fish in each aquarium. Children also are asked to add a two-digit and a one-digit number.

Task D-2   Pet Count
Children are asked to use doubles to solve a problem about the number of pets in the pet shop. Children also are asked to find half of a group and explain their answers.

Task D-3   It's for the Birds
Children are asked to add and subtract two-digit numbers, find ways that twelve can be divided into equal groups, and show their work.

Task D-4   Pet Store Animals
Children are asked to count tally marks, answer questions about a table, show their work, and write to explain their answers.

Name_____ Date _____

Pet Store

Task	Performance Indicators	Score (One score per task)
D-1	_____ finds two ways to separate 12 items into two equal groups _____ finds the sum $12 + 7$ _____ shows how to find the sum	3 2 1 0
D-2	_____ uses doubles to find the correct sum and draws a picture to show the doubles _____ finds half of a group, draws a picture, and writes the number _____ finds the total number of animals and shows how to find the sum	3 2 1 0
D-3	_____ subtracts $25 - 12$ correctly _____ adds $50 + 13$ correctly _____ identifies a way to separate 12 items into equal groups	3 2 1 0
D-4	_____ counts tally marks and writes the correct total _____ correctly answers questions about the table _____ explains why answers are correct	3 2 1 0
	Total Score _____/12	

Teaching Plan
Pet Store

Purpose

To assess the concepts, skills, and strategies that children have learned in Chapters 25–28

Task D-1 Lots of Fish!

Read the following to guide children through the task.

> The pet store has 12 fish. The pet store wants to put an equal number of fish in each of two aquariums. Show two ways the kinds of fish might be divided. You need to show an equal number of fish in each aquarium.

> The pet store receives 7 more fish. How many fish does the pet store have now? Show your work.

Task D-2 Pet Count

Ask children to name some of the pets they might see in a pet store. Then read the following to guide children through the task.

> The pet store has 4 dogs. The pet store has twice as many cats as dogs. How many cats does the pet store have? Show how you got your answer.

> The pet store has half as many birds as dogs. How many birds does the pet store have?

> How many pets does the store have in all? Show how you got your answers.

Encourage each child to draw his or her own picture and show that there is the correct number of each pet in each pen.

Task D-3 It's for the Birds

Read the following to guide children through the task.

> Mr. Tweetsie goes to the pet shop to buy birdseed. The store has 25 pounds of birdseed. Mr. Tweetsie buys 12 pounds of seed. How many pounds of seed does the store have left? Show how you know.

> The store gets 50 more pounds of seed. How many pounds does the store have now? Show how you know.

> Mr. Tweetsie goes home with his 12 pounds of seed. He fills his bird feeders with equal amounts of seed. How many bird feeders might he have? Show how you know.

Task D-4 Pet Store Animals

Ask students to name their favorite pet. Then read the following to guide children through the task.

> Look at the table. It shows the number of animals the pet store has. Fill in the table to show the number of each kind of pet. Which pet is there the most of?

> Which pet is there the least of?

> Do most pets in the store have 0 legs, 2 legs, or 4 legs? Tell how you know.

Name_____

Lots of Fish!

The pet store has 12 fish.

An equal number of fish is placed in each ☐. Show 2 ways the kinds of fish might be divided.

Aquarium 1

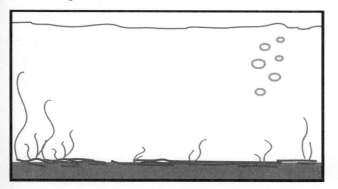

Aquarium 2

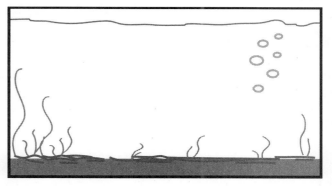

Aquarium 1

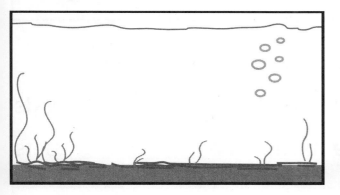

Aquarium 2

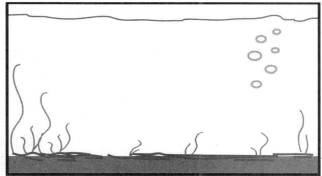

The pet store receives 7 more fish.
How many fish does the pet store have now? _____ fish

Show your work.

Pet Store D–1

Pet Count

The pet store has 4 dogs.

The pet store has <u>twice</u> as many 🐱 cats as 🐕 dogs.

How many <u>cats</u> does the pet store have? _____ cats

Show how you got your answer.

The pet store has <u>half</u> as many 🐦 birds as 🐕 dogs.

How many <u>birds</u> does the pet store have? _____ birds

How many <u>pets</u> does the store have in all? _____ pets

Show how you got your answers.

It's for the Birds

Mr. Tweetsie goes to the pet shop to buy birdseed. The store had 25 pounds of birdseed. Mr. Tweetsie buys 12 pounds of seed.

How many pounds of seed does the store have left? _____ pounds

Show how you know.

The store gets 50 more pounds of seed. How many pounds does the store have now? _____ pounds

Show how you know.

Mr. Tweetsie goes home with his 12 pounds of seed. He fills his bird feeders with equal amounts of seed.

How many bird feeders might he have? _____ feeders

Show how you know.

Pet Store Animals

Pets Sold Per Month

Pets	Number of Pets	Total
dog	⊪⊪ ‖	
cat	⊪⊪ ‖‖	
fish	⊪⊪ ⊪⊪ ⊪⊪ ‖‖	
snake	‖‖	
bird	⊪⊪ ⊪⊪ ⊪⊪ ‖	

Fill in the table to show how many pets there are.

Which pet is there the most of? _____

Which pet is there the least of? _____

Do most pets at the store have 0 legs, 2 legs,

or 4 legs? _____

Show how you got your answers.

Tell how you know.

_____

_____

Pet Store

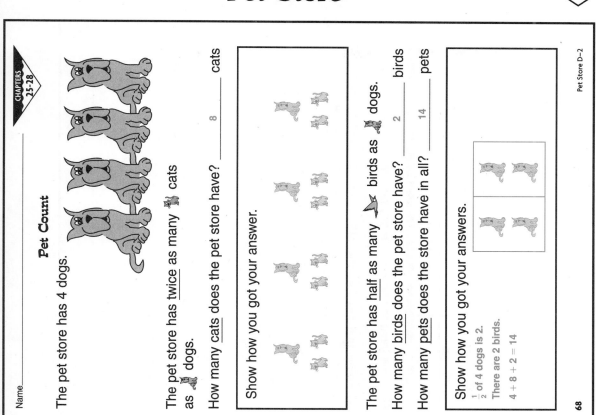

Name _____

Pet Count

The pet store has 4 dogs.

The pet store has twice as many cats as dogs.

How many cats does the pet store have? ___8___ cats

Show how you got your answer.

The pet store has half as many birds as dogs.

How many birds does the pet store have? ___2___ birds

How many pets does the store have in all? ___14___ pets

Show how you got your answers.

$\frac{1}{2}$ of 4 dogs is 2.
There are 2 birds.
$4 + 8 + 2 = 14$

68   Pet Store D–2

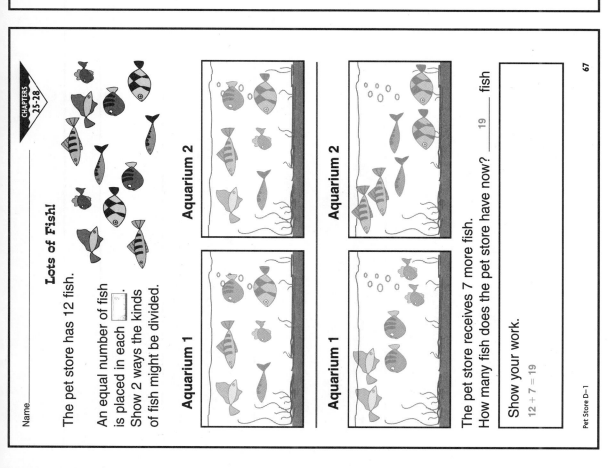

Name _____

Lots of Fish!

The pet store has 12 fish.

An equal number of fish is placed in each _____.
Show 2 ways the kinds of fish might be divided.

Aquarium 1

Aquarium 2

Aquarium 1

Aquarium 2

The pet store receives 7 more fish.
How many fish does the pet store have now? ___19___ fish

Show your work.

$12 + 7 = 19$

Pet Store D–1   67

Name

CHAPTERS 25-28

Pet Store Animals
Pets Sold Per Month

Pets		Number of Pets	Total
dog		|||| ||	7
cat		|||| |||	8
fish		|||| |||| |||	18
snake		|||	3
bird		|||| |||| ||	17

Fill in the table to show how many pets there are.

Which pet is there the most of? __fish__

Which pet is there the least of? __snake__

Do most pets at the store have 0 legs, 2 legs,
or 4 legs? __0 legs__

Show how you got your answers.

21 have 0 legs.

17 have 2 legs.

(7 + 8 = 15) have 4 legs.

Tell how you know.

Fish and snakes have 0 legs. 18 + 3 = 21; Birds have 2 legs. There are 17 birds.

Dogs and cats have 4 legs. 7 + 8 = 15

70   Pet Store D-4

Name

CHAPTERS 25-28

It's for the Birds

Mr. Tweetsie goes to the pet
shop to buy birdseed. The
store had 25 pounds of
birdseed. Mr. Tweetsie
buys 12 pounds of seed.

How many pounds of seed does the
store have left? __13__ pounds

Show how you know.

25 − 12 = 13

The store gets 50 more pounds of seed. How many
pounds does the store have now? __63__ pounds

Show how you know.

50 + 13 = 63

Mr. Tweetsie goes home with his 12 pounds of seed.
He fills his bird feeders with equal amounts of seed.

How many bird feeders might he have? __4__ feeders

Show how you know. Answers will vary.

x x x   x x x   x x x   x x x

He could have 4 bird feeders. Each feeder has 3 pounds.

Pet Store D-3   69

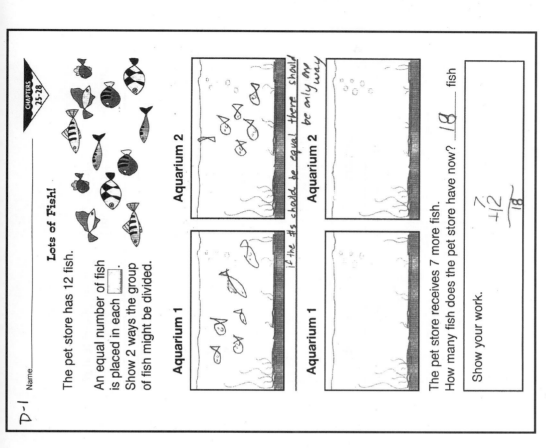

D-1

Name _____

Lots of Fish!

The pet store has 12 fish.

An equal number of fish
is placed in each [   ].
Show 2 ways the group
of fish might be divided.

Aquarium 1   Aquarium 2

if the #s should be equal there should
be only one way

Aquarium 1   Aquarium 2

The pet store receives 7 more fish.
How many fish does the pet store have now? _18_ fish

Show your work.

7
+12
18

Level 2   The child has successfully completed part of the task and
showed one way to group the fish. However, the child has added
incorrectly.

D-1

Name _____

Lots of Fish!

The pet store has 12 fish.

An equal number of fish
is placed in each [   ].
Show 2 ways the group
of fish might be divided.

Aquarium 1   Aquarium 2

Aquarium 1   Aquarium 2

The pet store receives 7 more fish.
How many fish does the pet store have now? _19_ fish

Show your work. I fig urd fi
out with my fingrs,

Pet Store D-1

Level 3   The child has successfully completed the task and found two
ways to group the fish equally. The child has also added correctly and
understood the task.

Model Student Papers for
Pet Store

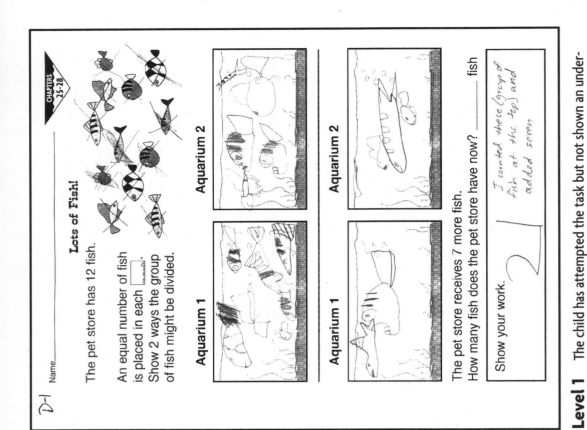

Level 1 The child has attempted the task but not shown an understanding of it. The child has also added incorrectly.

TEACHER NOTES

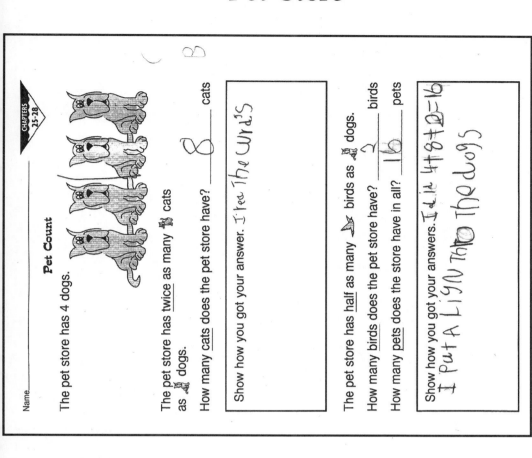

Left paper (Level 3):

Name_____

Pet Count

The pet store has 4 dogs.

CHAPTERS 25-28

The pet store has twice as many 🐱 cats as 🐕 dogs.

How many cats does the pet store have? ___ 8 cats

Show how you got your answer. 4+4 and
4 × 2 = 8.

The pet store has half as many 🐦 birds as 🐕 dogs.

How many birds does the pet store have? 2 birds

How many pets does the store have in all? 14 pets

Show how you got your answers. 4÷2 = 2
And thats half.
8+4 is 12 and 12+2=14

Level 3 The child has successfully completed all aspects of the task and showed an understanding of the concepts of twice as many and half.

Right paper (Level 2):

Name_____

Pet Count

The pet store has 4 dogs.

CHAPTERS 25-28

The pet store has twice as many 🐱 cats as 🐕 dogs.

How many cats does the pet store have? ___ 8 cats

Show how you got your answer. I ked the cwrd 15

The pet store has half as many 🐦 birds as 🐕 dogs.

How many birds does the pet store have? 2 birds

How many pets does the store have in all? 16 pets

Show how you got your answers. I did 4+8+2=16
I put a Lign thro the dogs

Level 2 The child has successfully completed part of the task, but has added incorrectly to find the total. The child's explanation shows an understanding of the concept.

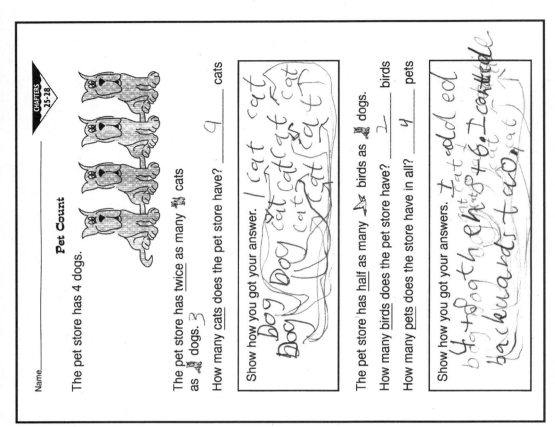

TEACHER NOTES

Level 1 The child has attempted all parts of the task. Answers to most parts are incorrect. The child demonstrates a very limited understanding of the task.

Level 2 Paper

CHAPTERS
25-28

Name _____

D-3

It's for the Birds

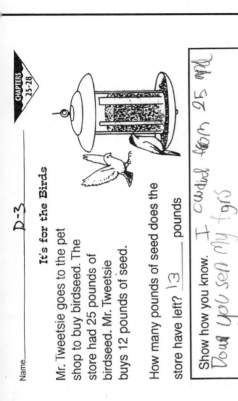

Mr. Tweetsie goes to the pet shop to buy birdseed. The store had 25 pounds of birdseed. Mr. Tweetsie buys 12 pounds of seed.

How many pounds of seed does the store have left? __13__ pounds

Show how you know. I cudul teen 25 mll Dow you sen ny tyrs

The store gets 50 more pounds of seed. How many pounds does the store have now? __75__ pounds

Show how you know. by the new Chot

Mr. Tweetsie goes home with his 12 pounds of seed. He fills his bird feeders with equal amounts of seed.

How many bird feeders might he have? __12__ feeders

Show how you know. I pon in each

Level 2 The child has successfully completed parts of the task. The child has used counting to subtract 12 from 25, and has been able to divide 12 into equal groups.

Level 3 Paper

Name _____

D-3

It's for the Birds

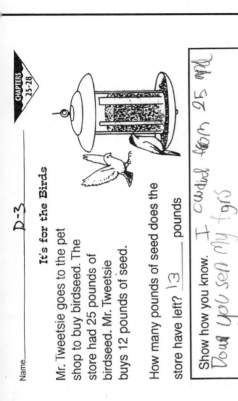

Mr. Tweetsie goes to the pet shop to buy birdseed. The store had 25 pounds of birdseed. Mr. Tweetsie buys 12 pounds of seed.

How many pounds of seed does the store have left? __13__ pounds

Show how you know. baecuus 25-12=13

The store gets 50 more pounds of seed. How many pounds does the store have now? __63__ pounds

Show how you know. baecaus 13+50 =63

Mr. Tweetsie goes home with his 12 pounds of seed. He fills his bird feeders with equal amounts of seed.

How many bird feeders might he have? __2__ feeders

Show how you know. he put 6 pounds of birdseed in eetch feeder

Level 3 The child has successfully completed all parts of the task, added and subtracted two-digit numbers correctly, and explained the answers given.

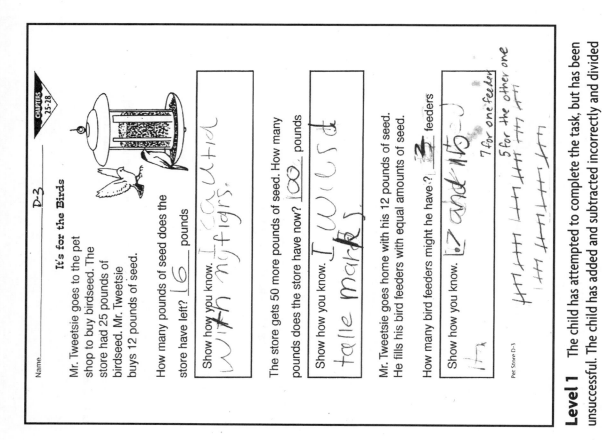

CHAPTERS
25-28

D-3

It's for the Birds

Name _____

Mr. Tweetsie goes to the pet shop to buy birdseed. The store had 25 pounds of birdseed. Mr. Tweetsie buys 12 pounds of seed.

How many pounds of seed does the store have left? __16__ pounds

Show how you know. I counted with my figars.

The store gets 50 more pounds of seed. How many pounds does the store have now? __100__ pounds

Show how you know. I will st talle marks.

Mr. Tweetsie goes home with his 12 pounds of seed. He fills his bird feeders with equal amounts of seed.

How many bird feeders might he have? __3__ feeders

Show how you know. 7 and 5

7 for one feeder
5 for the other one

Pet Store D-3

Level 1 The child has attempted to complete the task, but has been unsuccessful. The child has added and subtracted incorrectly and divided 12 into two groups that are unequal.

TEACHER NOTES

Model Student Papers for
Pet Store

Name _____

Pet Store Animals
Pets Sold Per Month

Pets	Number of Pets	Total
dog	✺ ||	7
cat	✺ |||	8
fish	✺ ✺ ✺ |||	18
snake	|||	3
bird	✺ ✺ ✺ ||	17

Fill in the table to show how many pets there are.

Which pet is there the most of? ___Bird and Fish___

Which pet is there the least of? ___Snake___

Do most pets at the store have 0 legs, 2 legs,
or 4 legs? ___0 legs___

Show how you got your answers.

||| 3   ✺ || 7
||||| 7   ✺ || 16
✺ |||| 16

Tell how you know.
BIRD snake + fish have 0 legs

Pet Store D-4

Level 2   The child has successfully completed parts of the task, but shows a lack of understanding of some of the concepts. The illustrations are irrelevant.

Name _____

Pet Store Animals
Pets Sold Per Month

Pets	Number of Pets	Total
dog	✺ ||	7
cat	✺ |||	8
fish	✺ ✺ ✺ |||	10
snake	|||	3
bird	✺ ✺ ||	17

Fill in the table to show how many pets there are.

Which pet is there the most of? ___fish___

Which pet is there the least of? ___snake___

Do most pets at the store have 0 legs, 2 legs,
or 4 legs? ___0 legs___

Show how you got your answers.
fish 18   dog 7   bird 17
cat 8   +
snake 3   15

Tell how you know.
I counted all the pets with 0
legs and got 2 pets.

Pet Store D-4

Level 3   The child has successfully completed the task. The computation and explanation given show an understanding of the concepts presented.

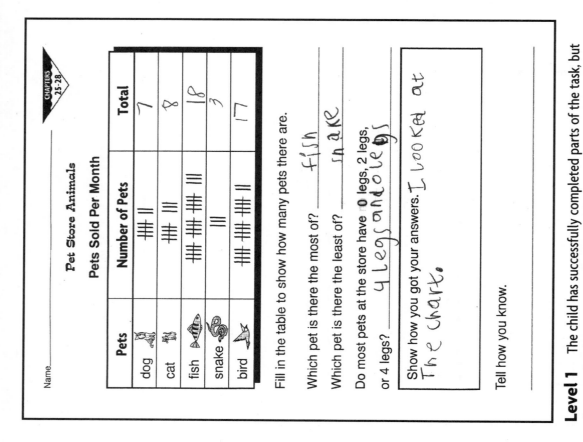

Name _____

Pet Store Animals

Pets Sold Per Month

Pets	Number of Pets	Total
dog	⊞ II	7
cat	⊞ III	8
fish	⊞ ⊞ ⊞ III	18
snake	III	3
bird	⊞ ⊞ II	17

Fill in the table to show how many pets there are.

Which pet is there the most of? ___fish___

Which pet is there the least of? ___snake___

Do most pets at the store have 0 legs, 2 legs,
or 4 legs? ___4 legs and 0 legs___

Show how you got your answers. I looked at
the chart.

Tell how you know. _____

TEACHER NOTES

Level 1 The child has successfully completed parts of the task, but does not develop a strategy to complete the task beyond that of looking at the chart.

Performance Assessment

Class Record Form

School	Assessment A					Assessment B				
	Task A-1	Task A-2	Task A-3	Task A-4	Total	Task B-1	Task B-2	Task B-3	Task B-4	Total
Teacher										
NAMES **Date**										

Performance Assessment

Class Record Form

School	Assessment C					Assessment D				
	Task C-1	Task C-2	Task C-3	Task C-4	Total	Task D-1	Task D-2	Task D-3	Task D-4	Total
Teacher										
NAMES **Date**										

► Evaluating Interview/Task Test Items

The interview/task test items are designed to provide an optional instrument to evaluate each child's level of accomplishment for each learning goal of the *Math Advantage* program. These items provide opportunities for children to verbalize or write about his or her thinking or to use manipulatives or other pictorial representations to represent their thinking. They test children at the concrete and pictorial levels, where appropriate, so that you can assess each child's progress toward functioning at the abstract level. The items will enable you to analyze the child's thought processes as they work on different types of problems and will enable you to plan instruction that will meet your children's needs.

You may wish to use these test items as you work through the content in the chapter to determine whether children are ready to move on or whether they need additional teaching or reinforcement activities. You may also wish to use these test items with children who did not successfully pass the chapter test to determine what types of reteaching activities are appropriate. These test items may also be used with students who have difficulty reading written material or who have learning disabilities.

The test items are designed to focus on evaluating how children think about mathematics and how they work at solving problems rather than on whether they can get the correct answer. The evaluation criteria given for each test item will help you pinpoint the errors in the children's thinking processes as they work through the problem.

A checklist of possible responses is provided to record each child's thinking processes. The Class Record Form can be used to show satisfactory completion of interview/task test items.

Materials: connecting cubes, picture of a group of 3 red balls and a group of 2 blue balls

TEST ITEM	EVALUATE WHETHER CHILD
1-A.1 *To use concrete materials to model addition story problems* Read the following story problem: There are 2 girls sitting at the table. There are 3 boys sitting at the table. How many children in all are sitting at the table? Have the child use cubes to model and solve the problem.	_____ uses 2 cubes to represent the girls and 3 cubes to represent the boys. _____ identifies the number of children sitting at the table as 5.
1-A.2 *To add 1 or 2 to find sums to 6* Show the child 3 cubes. Have the child show 1 more cube and name the sum for 3 + 1. Then show 4 cubes. Have the child show 2 more cubes and name the sum for 4 + 2.	_____ shows the correct number of cubes. _____ identifies the sums as 4 and 6.
1-A.3 *To use pictures to find sums* Show child a picture of 3 red balls and 2 blue balls. Have the child use the picture to find the sum for 3 + 2.	_____ writes an addition sentence for the picture. _____ identifies the sum as 5.
1-A.4 *To write and solve addition sentences to represent addition story problems* Show the child 1 red cube and 2 blue cubes. Have the child write an addition sentence to show how many cubes there are in all.	_____ writes an addition sentence for the number of cubes: $1 + 2 = $ ___. _____ identifies the sum as 3.

Evaluation of Interview/Task Test

Date _____

Child's Name_____

Materials: cubes, counters, picture of 5 balls with last 2 crossed out

TEST ITEM	EVALUATE WHETHER CHILD
2-A.1 *To use concrete materials to model subtraction story problems* Read the following story problem: There are 5 ducks on a pond. 3 ducks swim away. How many ducks are left? Have the child use cubes to model and solve the problem.	_____ first uses 5 cubes to represent the ducks on the pond and then moves away 3 cubes to show ducks swimming away. _____ identifies the number of ducks left as 2.
2-A.2 *To subtract 1 or 2 to find differences from 6* Show the child 4 counters. Have the child move away 1 counter and tell how many are left: $4 - 1 =$ ____. Then show 6 counters. Have the child move away 2 counters and tell how many are left: $6 - 2 =$ ____.	_____ moves away the correct number of counters. _____ identifies the differences as 3 and 4.
2-A.3 *To write subtraction sentences to represent pictures* Show the child a picture of 5 balls in a row with an X drawn on each of the last two balls. Have the child tell a story about the picture and write a subtraction sentence that shows the difference.	_____ tells a subtraction story about the pictures. _____ writes the subtraction sentence for the difference as $5 - 2 = 3$. _____ identifies the difference as 3.
2-A.4 *To use the strategy **make a model** to solve addition and subtraction story problems* Read the following story problems: 4 birds are on a branch. 1 bird flies away. How many birds are left? 4 birds are on a branch. 2 more birds come. How many birds in all? Have the child explain how to decide whether to add or subtract to solve each problem. Then have the child use counters to model and solve the problems.	for the first problem: _____ indicates subtraction because one bird is going away. _____ shows 4 counters and moves away one counter. _____ identifies the difference as 3. for the second problem: _____ indicates addition because one group of 2 birds is joining the group of 4. _____ shows 4 counters and adds 2 counters. _____ identifies the sum as 6.

Evaluation of Interview/Task Test

Date _____

Child's Name _____

Materials: two-color counters, dominoes or dot cards (TR 21), pennies

TEST ITEM	EVALUATE WHETHER CHILD
3-A.1 *To use a model or picture to explain the Commutative Property of addition* Have the child show a row with 1 yellow counter and 3 red counters. Next to this row, have the child show a row with 3 red counters and 1 yellow counter. Y R R R R R R Y Have the child explain how the model is alike and how it is different.	_____ shows the correct number and color of counters in each row. _____ explains that the sums are the same because there are the same number of yellow and red counters in each row. Just the order is different.
3-A.2 *To identify combinations of addends with sums to 10* Give the child 7 two-color counters. Have the child use the counters to show ways to make a sum of 7. Have the child write or tell the ways he or she found.	_____ uses the counters to show pairs of addends with a sum of 7. _____ uses the Commutative Property to identify pairs of addends with a sum of 7. _____ identifies the ways as $7 + 0, 6 + 1, 5 + 2, 4 + 3, 3 + 4, 2 + 5, 1 + 6, 0 + 7$.
3-A.3 *To add basic facts to 10 in vertical and horizontal formats* Show the child a domino in a horizontal position. Have the child write an addition sentence for the dots on the domino. Show the child the same domino in a vertical position. Have the child write and solve a vertical addition problem for the dots on the domino.	_____ writes the horizontal addition sentence as $3 + 5 = 8$. _____ writes the vertical addition problem as: $$\begin{array}{r} 3 \\ + 5 \\ \hline 8 \end{array}$$
3-A.4 *To use the strategy **make a model** to solve addition problems with money* Have the child choose any two toys on pages 65 and 66 and use pennies to show the price of each toy. Then have the child find the total amount.	_____ shows the correct number of pennies for each toy. _____ identifies the correct total amount for both toys.

Performance Assessment

Evaluation of Interview/Task Test

Date _____

Child's Name _____

Materials: connecting cubes, counters

TEST ITEM	EVALUATE WHETHER CHILD
4-A.1 *To use the **counting on** strategy to add* Show the child a train of 6 connecting cubes, and explain that there are 6 cubes in the train. Then show the child 3 loose cubes. Have the child count on from 6 to find out how many cubes there are in all. Then have the child name the sum in an addition sentence: $6 + 3 = $ ___.	_____ counts on from 6 correctly: 6 . . . 7, 8, 9. _____ identifies the sum as 9.
4-A.2 *To use counters to show and write **doubles** facts* Place 4 counters in a group. Have the child use counters to make another group to show doubles. Then have child write the doubles fact.	_____ shows another group of 4 counters. _____ writes the doubles fact as $4 + 4 = 8$.
4-A.3 *To find sums to 10* Write these problems on cards or paper: $6 + 1 = $ ___ $7 + 2 = $ ___ $5 + 5 = $ ___ Have the child name a way to find each sum and then give the sum.	_____ names a strategy that could be used to solve each problem; for example, $6 + 1 = $ ___ → counting on. $7 + 2 = $ ___ → counting on. $5 + 5 = $ ___ → doubles. _____ identifies the sums as 7, 9, and 10.
4-A.4 *To use the strategy **draw a picture** to solve story problems* Read the following story problems. Have the child tell whether he or she would add or subtract to solve each problem and explain why. Then have the child draw pictures to solve the problems. Aaron has 6 cookies. He eats 3 cookies. How many cookies are left? Amy has 3 red apples. She has 2 green apples. How many apples does Amy have in all?	for the first problem: _____ indicates subtraction because some of the cookies are being eaten. _____ draws an appropriate picture. _____ identifies the difference as 3. for the second problem: _____ indicates addition because she is getting more apples. _____ draws an appropriate picture. _____ identifies the sum as 5.

Child's Name _____

Materials: connecting cubes, counters, picture of a row of 9 circles with the last 3 crossed out

TEST ITEM	EVALUATE WHETHER CHILD
5-A.1 *To identify combinations of ways to subtract from numbers 10 or less* Give the child 8 counters. Have the child use the counters to show ways to subtract from 8. Have the child write or tell the ways he or she found.	_____ uses the counters to show how he or she can begin with 8 and then take away 0, 1, 2, 3, 4, 5, 6, 7, or 8. _____ identifies the ways as $8 - 0 = 8$, $8 - 1 = 7$, $8 - 2 = 6$, $8 - 3 = 5$, $8 - 4 = 4$, $8 - 5 = 3$, $8 - 6 = 2$, $8 - 7 = 1$, $8 - 8 = 0$.
5-A.2 *To subtract in horizontal and vertical formats* Show the child a picture of a row of 9 identical circles with an X drawn on each of the last 3 circles. Have the child write a subtraction sentence for the circles. Turn the picture of the circles so that they are in a vertical column. Have the child write and solve a vertical subtraction problem for the circles.	_____ writes the horizontal addition sentence as $9 - 3 = 6$. _____ writes the vertical subtraction problem as: $$\begin{array}{r} 9 \\ -\,3 \\ \hline 6 \end{array}$$
5-A.3 *To identify fact families with sums to 10* Give the child a cube train of 5 red cubes and 4 blue cubes, and have the child write or tell the two addition sentences shown by the train. Then have the child break apart the cube train into a train of red cubes and a train of blue cubes and write or tell the two subtraction sentences shown by the trains. Finally, have the child name the three numbers in the fact family.	_____ identifies the two addition sentences as $5 + 4 = 9$ and $4 + 5 = 9$. _____ identifies the two subtraction sentences as $9 - 4 = 5$ and $9 - 5 = 4$. _____ identifies the three numbers in the fact family as 4, 5, and 9.
5-A.4 *To use subtraction to compare two groups of 10 or less* Give the child 8 red counters and 6 yellow counters. Have the child match the red counters with the yellow counters and tell how many more red counters than yellow counters there are.	_____ sets up the red and yellow counters with 1 to 1 correspondence. _____ states that there are 2 more red counters than yellow counters.

Materials: number line for 0 to 10

TEST ITEM	EVALUATE WHETHER CHILD
6-A.1 *To use the **counting back** strategy to subtract* Show the child a number line for 0 to 10. Have the child count back on the number line to subtract $7 - 3$ and $8 - 2$.	_____ counts back on the number line correctly. _____ identifies the differences as 4 and 6.
6-A.2 *To subtract zero and subtract to find a difference of zero* Have the child draw 8 circles on paper and then cross out circles to show how many are taken away. Have the child tell how many are left for these subtraction sentences: $8 - 0$ and $8 - 8$.	_____ crosses out 0 circles for $8 - 0$. _____ crosses out 8 circles for $8 - 8$. _____ identifies the differences as 8 and 0.
6-A.3 *To find sums and differences for addition and subtraction facts to 10* Write these problems on cards or paper: $9 - 2 = $ ___ $5 - 0 = $ ___ $8 - 4 = $ ___ Have the child name a way to find each difference and then give the difference.	_____ names a strategy that could be used to solve each fact; for example, $9 - 2 = $ ___ $\rightarrow$ counting back. $5 - 0 = $ ___ $\rightarrow$ subtracting zero. $8 - 4 = $ ___ $\rightarrow$ doubles. _____ identifies the differences as 7, 5, and 4.
6-A.4 *To use the strategy **drawing a picture** to solve problems* Read the following story problems: 4 ducks are swimming in a pond. 2 more come. How many are in the pond now? 5 birds sing in a tree. 1 flies away. How many are in the tree now? Have the child tell whether he or she would add or subtract to solve each problem and why. Then have the child draw pictures to solve the problems.	for the first problem: _____ indicates addition because some ducks are coming to join ducks already in the pond. _____ draws an appropriate picture. _____ identifies the sum as 6. for the second problem: _____ indicates subtraction because 1 of the 5 birds is flying away. _____ draws an appropriate picture. _____ identifies the difference as 4.

Evaluation of Interview/Task Test

Date _____

Child's Name _____

Materials: solid figures: sphere, rectangular prism, cone, cylinder, cubes, and pyramid

TEST ITEM	EVALUATE WHETHER CHILD
7-A.1 *To identify real objects that are shaped like solid figures* Display a set of solid figures that includes a sphere, rectangular prism, cone, cylinder, cube, and pyramid. For each figure, have the child name an object in the classroom (or at home) that has the same shape.	identifies an appropriate object for each figure: _____ sphere _____ rectangular prism _____ cone _____ cylinder _____ cube _____ pyramid
7-A.2 *To sort solid figures by attributes or properties* Display a set of solid figures that includes a sphere, rectangular prism, cone, cylinder, cube, and pyramid. Have the child point to the figures that will stack, will roll, and will slide. Then have the child point to the figures with no flat faces, 1 flat face, 2 flat faces, and all flat faces.	identifies figures that will _____ stack (cube, rectangular prism, cylinder). _____ roll (sphere, cone, cylinder). _____ slide (cube, cone, rectangular prism, pyramid, cylinder). identifies figures that have _____ no flat faces (sphere). _____ 1 flat face (cone). _____ 2 flat faces (cylinder). _____ all flat faces (rectangular prism, cube, pyramid).
7-A.3 *To use the strategy* **make a model** *to identify how many cubes are used to build a model* Build a model using 12 or fewer cubes. (See pupil pages 129–130.) Have the child use cubes to build a model like the one you made. Then have the child tell how many cubes the model contains.	_____ builds a model like the given model. _____ correctly identifies the number of cubes that the model contains.

Performance Assessment

Evaluation of Interview/Task Test   Date _____

CHAPTER 8

Materials: solid figures: sphere, rectangular prism, cone, cylinder, cube, and triangular pyramid; geoboard or dot paper; construction-paper square

TEST ITEM	EVALUATE WHETHER CHILD
8-A.1 *To identify plane figures* Display a set of solid shapes that includes a rectangular prism, cylinder, cube, and triangular pyramid. Have the child identify the shapes of the flat faces on each solid figure.	_____ identifies the flat faces on the rectangular prism as rectangles. _____ identifies the flat faces on the cylinder as circles. _____ identifies the flat faces on the cube as squares. _____ identifies the flat faces on the triangular pyramid as triangles.
8-A.2 *To sort plane figures by the number of sides and corners* Show the child a triangle and a square. Have the child tell how many sides and corners each figure has.	_____ states that the triangle has 3 sides and 3 corners. _____ states that the square has 4 sides and 4 corners.
8-A.3 *To identify figures that have the same size and shape* Show the child a square or a triangle on a geoboard or on dot paper. Have the child make a figure that is the same size and shape as yours on another geoboard or on dot paper. Have the child explain how he or she knows that the figures are the same size and shape.	_____ makes a figure that is the same size and shape as your figure. _____ explains how he or she knows that the figures are the same size and shape.
8-A.4 *To identify a line of symmetry in plane figures* Give the child a construction-paper square. Have the child fold the paper (or draw a line) to show a line of symmetry. Have the child explain how he or she knows that the line is a line of symmetry.	_____ folds the square in half or draws a line to show a line of symmetry. _____ explains how he or she knows that the line is a line of symmetry.

Evaluation of Interview/Task Test

Date _____

Child's Name _____

Materials: crayons, 3/4-inch grid paper (TR 90)

TEST ITEM	EVALUATE WHETHER CHILD
9-A.1 *To identify plane figures as open or closed* Have the child draw an open figure and a closed figure. Have the child explain how the figures are different.	_____ draws an open figure. _____ draws a closed figure. _____ explains how the figures are different.
9-A.2 *To classify objects by position* Have the child draw a circle on paper. Have the child draw a red X on the circle, a blue X inside the circle, and a green X outside the circle. Then have the child draw a black bug to the left of the circle and a yellow bug to the right of the circle.	_____ correctly draws the colored X's inside, outside, and on the circle. _____ correctly draws the colored bugs to the right and left of the circle.
9-A.3 *To locate positions on a grid* Show the child a grid like the one on pupil page 154. Have the child follow these directions: Go 3 right and 4 up. Draw a circle. Go 5 right and 2 up. Draw a triangle.	_____ locates the correct position on the grid for 3 right and 4 up and draws a circle. _____ locates the correct position on the grid for 5 right and 2 up and draws a triangle.

Evaluation of Interview/Task Test

Date _____

CHAPTER 10

Child's Name _____

Materials: connecting cubes, attribute shapes or construction-paper shapes

TEST ITEM	EVALUATE WHETHER CHILD
10-A.1 *To identify, describe, reproduce, and extend patterns* Use connecting cubes to create these patterns: • red, green, green, red, green, green, red, green, green • red, green, blue, red, green, blue, red, green, blue Have the child describe the patterns by naming the colors. Then have the child copy the patterns with connecting cubes. Finally, have the child add 3 more blocks to extend each pattern.	_____ identifies the patterns by naming the colors. _____ copies the patterns correctly. _____ continues the first pattern by adding red, green, green. _____ extends the second pattern by adding red, green, blue.
10-A.2 *To create patterns* Show the child the following pattern made from construction-paper shapes: • red square, red circle, red square, red circle, red square, red circle Have the child use 4 more shapes to continue the pattern. Then have the child use the same shapes to show a new pattern.	_____ extends the pattern correctly by adding red square, red circle, red square, red circle. _____ uses the shapes to create a new pattern; for example, red circle, red circle, red square, red circle, red circle, red square, red circle, red circle, red square.
10-A.3 *To analyze and correct patterns* Show the child the following pattern made from attribute shapes or construction-paper shapes: • square, circle, square, circle, square, triangle, square, circle Have the child find and correct the mistake in the pattern.	_____ correctly identifies the mistake in the pattern (triangle should be a circle). _____ corrects the mistake by replacing the triangle with a circle.

Evaluation of Interview/Task Test

Date _____

Child's Name _____

Materials: connecting cubes, small box

TEST ITEM	EVALUATE WHETHER CHILD
11-A.1 *To use strategies such as counting on and doubles to find sums to 12* Write these problems on cards or paper: 7 + 1 = ___ 2 + 9 = ___ 6 + 6 = ___ Have the child name a way to find each sum and then give the sum.	_____ explains a strategy that could be used to solve each problem; for example, 7 + 1 = ___ → counting on. 2 + 9 = ___ → counting on. 6 + 6 = ___ → doubles. _____ identifies the sums as 8, 11, and 12.
11-A.2 *To add three addends with sums through 12* Write this problem on paper: 3 + 2 + 5 = ___. Have the child explain how he or she would find the sum and then give the sum. Then ask the child to show another way the problem could be solved and then solve it.	_____ explains that he or she would find the sum by adding the first two numbers (3 + 2 = 5) and then adding this sum to the third number (5 + 5 = 10). _____ explains that he or she could also find the sum by adding the (5 + 2 = 7) and then adding this sum to the third number (3 + 7 = 10). _____ identifies the sum as 10 using both methods.
11-A.3 *To solve addition problems by acting them out and writing addition sentences to represent the problems* Read the following story problem: Jill put 3 red cubes in a box. Then she put 8 blue cubes in the box. How many cubes were in the box? Have the child act out the problem by putting cubes in a box. Have the child write an addition sentence to represent the problem.	_____ puts the correct number of red and blue cubes in the box. _____ identifies the total number of cubes in the box as 11. _____ writes an addition sentence to represent the problem (3 + 8 = 11).

TEST ITEM	EVALUATE WHETHER CHILD
12-A.1 *To use mental math strategies to find differences to 12* Write these problems on paper: $11 - 3 =$ ____ $12 - 6 =$ ____ $10 - 8 =$ ____ Have the child explain how he or she would find each difference and then give the difference.	_____ names a strategy (such as relating addition and subtraction, counting back, doubles, or fact families) that could be used to solve each problem. _____ identifies the differences as 8, 6, and 2.
12-A.2 *To compare groups of objects to find the differences between them* Give the child 11 red counters and 7 yellow counters. Have the child match the red counters with the yellow counters and tell how many more red counters than yellow counters there are.	_____ matches the red counters and the yellow counters. _____ states that there are 4 more red counters than yellow counters.
12-A.3 *To solve addition and subtraction story problems by writing a number sentence* Read the following story problems: There are 11 dogs in the pet store. There are 8 cats in the pet store. How many more dogs than cats are there? There are 7 blue birds. There are 5 red birds. How many birds are there in all? Have the child tell whether he or she would add or subtract to solve each problem. Then have the child write an addition sentence or a subtraction sentence to represent the problem and tell its answer.	for the first problem: _____ indicates subtraction because two groups are being compared. After you match each dog with a cat, there are 3 dogs left over. _____ identifies that there are 3 more dogs than cats. _____ writes an appropriate subtraction sentence for the problem: $11 - 8 = 3$. for the second problem: _____ indicates addition because you are joining a group of blue birds with a group of red birds. _____ identifies that there are 12 birds in all. _____ writes an appropriate addition sentence for the problem: $7 + 5 = 12$.

Child's Name _____

Materials: beansticks and beans or connecting cubes, counters

TEST ITEM	EVALUATE WHETHER CHILD
13-A.1 *To count groups of tens and identify and write the number* Have the child use beansticks (or 10-cube trains) to represent 20 and 80. For each number, have the child tell how many tens and say the number.	for 20: _____ indicates that there are 2 tens. _____ indicates that the number is 20. for 80: _____ indicates that there are 8 tens. _____ indicates that the number is 80.
13-A.2 *To count groups of tens and ones to 100 and identify and write the number* Give the child beansticks and beans (or 10-cube trains and cubes) to represent 37 and 73 (or any pair of reversed numbers between 11 and 99). For each number, have the child tell how many tens and ones and say the number.	for 37: _____ indicates that there are 3 tens and 7 ones. _____ indicates that the number is 37. for 73: _____ indicates that there are 7 tens and 3 ones. _____ indicates that the number is 73.
13-A.3 *To use 10 as a benchmark to estimate a quantity as more than or fewer than 10* Show the child a group of 10 counters and identify the group as having 10. Then show the child groups of 6 counters, 19 counters, and 8 counters. Have the child estimate without counters whether there are fewer than 10 or more than 10 counters in each group.	_____ estimates that there are fewer than 10 counters in the groups with 6 and 8 counters. _____ estimates that there are more than 10 counters in the group with 19 counters.

Materials: connecting cubes, base-ten blocks

TEST ITEM	EVALUATE WHETHER CHILD
14-A.1 *To identify ordinal numbers from first through twelfth* Make a 12-cube train. The first cube should be red; all the other cubes should be blue. Place the cube train in front of the child with the red cube to the left. Tell the child that the red cube is *first*. Have the child tell the position of each blue cube.	_____ correctly identifies the ordinal number for each cube.
14-A.2 *To compare two numbers and identify which number is greater or less* Have the child use base-ten models for 32 and 26. Then have the child explain how to compare the models to determine which number is greater and which number is less.	_____ models the numbers correctly. _____ explains that 32 is the greater number because 32 has more tens than 26.
14-A.3 *To identify numbers that come before, after, or between other numbers* Have the child name and write a number between 12 and 99. Then have the child name and write the number that comes before it and the number that comes after it. Write on paper 45 and 47 or other numbers that differ by 2. Have the child name and write the number that comes between the two numbers.	_____ identifies the number before the given number. _____ identifies the number after the given number. _____ identifies the number between the two given numbers.
14-A.4 *To order numbers (less than 100) from least to greatest or from greatest to least* Write these numbers on paper: 71, 85, 63. Have the child explain how to order the numbers from least to greatest or from greatest to least. Then have the child write the numbers in order from least to greatest and in order from greatest to least.	_____ explains that when ordering from least to greatest, you write the number with the least number of tens first and the number with the greatest number of tens last. _____ explains that when ordering from greatest to least, you write the number with the greatest number of tens first and the number with the least number of tens last. _____ writes the numbers from least to greatest as 63, 71, 85. _____ writes the numbers from greatest to least as 85, 71, 63.

Evaluation of Interview/Task Test

Date _____

Child's Name _____

Materials: connecting cubes

TEST ITEM	EVALUATE WHETHER CHILD
15-A.1 *To count by twos, fives, and tens to 100* Have the child count by twos from 2 to 100, by fives from 5 to 100, and by tens from 10 to 100.	_____ counts by twos correctly. _____ counts by fives correctly. _____ counts by tens correctly.
15-A.2 *To identify a number as even or odd* Have the child use cubes to show whether the number 15 is an even number or an odd number. Then have him or her repeat the task for the number 12.	_____ either aligns the cubes in two rows or snaps them together in pairs to show whether the numbers are even or odd. _____ identifies 15 as an odd number. _____ identifies 12 as an even number.

aterials: coins (pennies, nickels, and dimes), small items with price tags of 15¢ and 21¢

TEST ITEM	EVALUATE WHETHER CHILD
16-A.1 *To count groups of pennies and groups of nickels and give the value* Give the child 8 pennies. Have the child count the pennies by ones and tell the number of cents. Then give the child 4 nickels. Have the child count the nickels by fives and tell the number of cents.	_____ counts the 8 pennies by ones. _____ identifies the value of the 8 pennies as 8¢. _____ counts the 4 nickels by fives. _____ identifies the value of the 4 nickels as 20¢.
16-A.2 *To count groups of dimes and give the value* Give the child 6 dimes. Have the child count the dimes by tens and tell the number of cents.	_____ counts the 6 dimes by tens. _____ identifies the value of the 6 dimes as 60¢.
16-A.3 *To count combinations of nickels and pennies and give the value* Give the child 3 nickels and 4 pennies. Have the child count the nickels by fives and count on the pennies by ones. Then have the child tell the number of cents.	_____ counts the 3 nickels by fives and counts on the 4 pennies by ones. _____ identifies the value of the group of coins as 19¢.
16-A.4 *To count combinations of dimes and pennies and give the value* Give the child 4 dimes and 3 pennies. Have the child count the dimes by tens and count on the pennies by ones. Then have the child tell the number of cents.	_____ counts the 4 dimes by tens and counts on the 3 pennies by ones. _____ identifies the value of the group of coins as 43¢.
16-A.5 *To use the strategy **make a model** to identify coins they could use to buy an object* Show the child items with price tags of 15¢ and 21¢. Have the child use coins (pennies, nickels, and dimes) to show the amount needed to buy each item.	_____ correctly identifies a combination of coins that equals 15¢. _____ correctly identifies a combination of coins that equals 21¢.

Evaluation of Interview/Task Test

Date _____

CHAPTER 17

Child's Name _____

Materials: coins (quarter, pennies, nickels, and dimes), various small toys with price tags

TEST ITEM	EVALUATE WHETHER CHILD
17-A.1 *To trade pennies for nickels and dimes* Give the child 15 pennies. Have the child trade the pennies for nickels and dimes.	_____ trades 10 pennies for 1 dime. _____ trades 5 pennies for 1 nickel. OR _____ trades 15 pennies for 3 nickels.
17-A.2 *To use combinations of coins to show a given amount using the fewest coins* Show the child an object on which you have placed a price tag of 30¢. Have the child show the price two different ways, using pennies, nickels, and dimes. Then have the child tell which way uses fewer coins.	_____ shows the amount correctly in two ways. _____ indicates which way uses fewer coins.
17-A.3 *To identify the coins needed to purchase an item* Show the child an object on which you have placed a price tag of 45¢. Have the child show the price using the fewest coins (pennies, nickels, dimes).	_____ uses the fewest coins to show 45¢ as 4 dimes and 1 nickel.
17-A.4 *To make combinations of pennies, nickels, and dimes that represent the value of a quarter* Show the child a quarter. Have the child show two combinations of pennies, nickels, and dimes that have the same value as a quarter.	_____ correctly shows two ways to use combinations of pennies, nickels, and dimes that have the same value as a quarter.

Materials: monthly calendar

TEST ITEM	EVALUATE WHETHER CHILD
18-A.1 *To read a calendar* Have the child look at a calendar for the current month and answer these questions about the calendar: • What is today's date? • What day was it yesterday? • How many Sundays are in this month?	_____ identifies today's date. _____ identifies the day of the week that was yesterday. _____ identifies the number of Sundays in the month.
18-A.2 *To sequence events* Have the child name 3 events that happened in one day or on 3 separate days and the order in which they happened. The child may use morning, afternoon, and evening or name days of the week on which the events happened.	_____ sequences three events in the correct order.
18-A.3 *To identify which of two tasks will take more time* Name the following pairs of activities: writing your name writing the letters of the alphabet eating a grape eating an apple Have the child tell which activity in each pair takes more time.	_____ identifies writing the letters of the alphabet as taking more time than writing your name. _____ identifies eating an apple as taking more time than eating a grape.

Evaluation of Interview/Task Test

Date _____

CHAPTER 19

Child's Name _____

Materials: analog clock, digital clock

TEST ITEM	EVALUATE WHETHER CHILD
19-A.1 *To tell time to the hour and half hour* Show these times on an analog clock and then a digital clock: 5:00, 8:30, 12:00. Have the child identify each time. Then name these times: 4:00, 10:00, 7:30. Have the child show the times on an analog clock and a digital clock.	identifies the times on the clock as: _____ 5:00. _____ 8:30. _____ 12:00. shows these times on the clock correctly: _____ 4:00. _____ 10:00. _____ 7:30.
19-A.2 *To estimate the time needed to do a task as more or less than one minute* Name some activities that take more than a minute and some activities that take less than a minute. Possible activities: • walking a dog • pouring a glass of milk • closing the classroom door • eating lunch Have the child tell whether each activity takes more than a minute or less than a minute.	_____ correctly identifies activities that take more than a minute. _____ correctly identifies activities that take less than a minute.

Performance Assessme

aterials: pencil, marker, paper clips, inch ruler, centimeter ruler

TEST ITEM	EVALUATE WHETHER CHILD
20-A.1 *To estimate and then measure the length of objects using nonstandard units* Give the child two classroom objects, such as a pencil and a marker. Have the child first estimate and then measure the length of each in paper clips.	_____ gives a reasonable estimate of the length in paper clips of each object. _____ correctly measures each object in paper clips.
20-A.2 *To estimate and then measure the length of objects in inches* Give the child two classroom objects, such as a pencil and a marker. Have the child first estimate and then measure the length of each object in inches.	_____ gives a reasonable estimate of the length in inches of each object. _____ correctly measures each object in inches.
20-A.3 *To estimate and then measure the length of objects in centimeters* Give the child two classroom objects, such as a pencil and a marker. Have the child first estimate and then measure the length of each object in centimeters.	_____ gives a reasonable estimate of the length in centimeters of each object. _____ correctly measures each object in centimeters.

Evaluation of Interview/Task Test

Date _____

CHAPTER 21

Child's Name _____

Materials: balance, cubes, board eraser, rice, measuring cup, quart container

TEST ITEM	EVALUATE WHETHER CHILD
21-A.1 *To estimate, then weigh, using a balance to determine which of two objects is heavier* Have the child first estimate and then use a balance to determine which of two classroom objects is heavier.	_____ gives a reasonable estimate as to which of the objects is heavier. _____ uses a balance correctly to determine which object is heavier.
21-A.2 *To estimate, then weigh, using nonstandard objects* Have the child first estimate and then use a balance to determine how many cubes it takes to balance a board eraser.	_____ gives a reasonable estimate of the number of cubes it will take to balance the eraser. _____ uses a balance correctly to determine the number of cubes it takes to balance the eraser.
21-A.3 *To estimate, then measure, about how many cups a container will hold* Give the child a quart container. Have the child first estimate and then measure to determine how many cups of rice the quart container will hold.	_____ gives a reasonable estimate of the number of cups of rice the quart container will hold. _____ correctly measures to determine that the quart container holds about 4 cups of rice.
21-A.4 *To classify the temperature of objects as hot or cold* Name several objects that are hot or cold. Possible objects: ice cubes, bowl of soup, mug of coffee, yogurt cone, campfire. Have the child describe each object as hot or cold. Then have the child name a hot object and a cold object.	_____ correctly identifies the named objects as hot or cold. _____ correctly names a hot object and a cold object.

aterials: index cards with fractions drawn or written on them, two-color counters

TEST ITEM	EVALUATE WHETHER CHILD
22-A.1 *To identify equal parts, halves, fourths, and thirds of a whole* Give the child six cards, on each of which you have drawn one circle. The 6 circles are divided respectively into 2, 3, and 4 equal parts and 2, 3, and 4 unequal parts. Have the child sort the cards into two groups, one for circles divided into equal parts and one for circles divided into unequal parts. Give the child six cards, on three of which you have drawn a square. The 3 squares are divided respectively into halves with $\frac{1}{2}$ shaded, thirds with $\frac{1}{3}$ shaded, and fourths with $\frac{1}{4}$ shaded. On each of the other three cards, write one of the following fractions: $\frac{1}{2}, \frac{1}{3}, \frac{1}{4}$. Have the child match each picture card with a fraction card and explain why the cards match.	_____ classifies the circles as divided into equal or unequal parts. _____ identifies halves, thirds, and fourths by matching the cards correctly. _____ explains that $\frac{1}{2}$ means 1 of 2 equal parts, $\frac{1}{3}$ means 1 of 3 equal parts, and $\frac{1}{4}$ means 1 of 4 equal parts.
22-A.2 *To visualize results of sharing equal parts to solve problems* Show the child the three cards with circles divided into 2, 3, and 4 equal parts. Read the following story to the child: There is one pizza for 4 children. Each child gets an equal share. How would you cut the pizza? Tell the child to pretend that the circles on the cards are pizzas divided into fair shares. Have the child choose the "pizza" that answers the question. Then have the child explain why he or she chose that card.	_____ chooses the card with the circle divided into fourths. _____ explains that the card shows 4 equal shares, one for each child.
22-A.3 *To identify equal parts of a group* Give the child a group of six counters. Have the child use the counters to make equal groups, such as two groups of 3. Then have the child put the counters together and try to make equal groups of another size, such as three groups of 2. Have the child explain how he or she knows the groups are equal.	_____ makes equal groups with the counters. _____ explains that there are the same number of counters in each group.

Materials: construction-paper shapes, small zip-type plastic bag, paper bag, connecting cubes, Tally Table (TR96)

TEST ITEM	EVALUATE WHETHER CHILD
23-A.1 *To sort objects and record data in a tally table* Give the child a blank tally table and a set of construction-paper shapes that can be sorted into two groups in different ways. Have the child sort the shapes into two groups and record the sorting in the tally table.	_____ sorts the shapes correctly into two groups. _____ completes the tally table correctly for the sorting.
23-A.2 *To use data to determine if an outcome is certain or impossible, and which of two events is most likely* Give the child a zip-type plastic bag containing the following cubes: 4 yellow, 3 red, 2 blue, 1 green. Name the following groups of cubes, and have the child tell whether they could or could not come out of the bag. • 2 red cubes • 3 green cubes • 1 yellow and 1 blue cube Remove the 1 green cube and the 3 red cubes from the bag. Ask the child: Would you be more likely to get a yellow cube or a blue cube from this bag? Then have the child explain why the chosen color is more likely.	_____ indicates that 2 red cubes and 1 yellow cube and 1 blue cube could come out of the bag. _____ indicates that 3 green cubes could not come out of the bag. _____ indicates that you are more likely to get a yellow cube. _____ explains that you are more likely to get yellow because there are more yellow cubes in the bag.
23-A.3 *To make predictions and record data in a tally table* Give the child a blank tally table and a paper bag containing 3 red cubes and 1 green cube. Have the child make a prediction about which color cube he or she will pull out most often if he or she takes a cube from the bag 10 times. Then have the child follow these steps 10 times: • Shake the bag. • Take a cube from the bag. • Make a tally mark in the table. • Put the cube back into the bag.	_____ predicts that he or she will pull out red more often. _____ does the activity and correctly records the results in the tally table.

valuation of Interview/Task Test

Date ____________

CHAPTER 24

ild's Name ______________________________

aterials: graph grid and tally table labeled as indicated, construction-paper shapes

TEST ITEM	EVALUATE WHETHER CHILD
24-A.1 *To record and interpret data in graphs* Give the child a graph grid (with circle, square, rectangle, and triangle as the labels for the rows) and the following construction-paper shapes: 1 triangle, 2 circles, 3 squares, and 4 rectangles. Have the child count the shapes and draw them to fill in the graph.	_______ draws the correct number of each shape. _______ draws the shapes in the correct row.
24-A.2 *To count, record, and interpret data in tally tables and bar graphs* Give the child a graph grid. Show the child a tally table with the following data on flowers: Flowers Total rose IIII 4 tulip II 2 daisy ~~IIII~~ I 6 Have the child use the data in the tally table to make a bar graph.	_______ labels the graph correctly with the names (or pictures) of the flowers. _______ draws bars of the correct length for each flower.

Evaluation of Interview/Task Test

Child's Name _____

Materials: index cards, counters, 8/8 domino or domino cards (TR21)

TEST ITEM	EVALUATE WHETHER CHILD
25-A.1 *To find sums to 18 using mental math strategies such as **doubles, doubles plus one,** and **doubles minus one*** Write these problems on index cards or paper: 7 + 7 = _____ 7 + 8 = _____ 7 + 6 = _____ Have the child name a way to find each sum and then give each sum.	_____ names a strategy that could be used to solve each problem; for example, 7 + 7 = ___ → doubles 7 + 8 = ___ → doubles plus one 7 + 6 = ___ → doubles minus one _____ identifies the sums as 14, 15, and 13.
25-A.2 *To write the related addition and subtraction number sentences for doubles fact families* Show the child an 8/8 domino or domino card. Have the child write the addition sentence for the dots on the domino. Then have the child write the related subtraction sentence.	_____ writes 8 + 8 = 16 as the addition sentence. _____ writes 16 − 8 = 8 as the related subtraction sentence.
25-A.3 *To solve story problems by **making a model*** Read the following story problems: I have 5 apples. My friend has the same number. How many apples do we have in all? Sue has some pennies. Jon gives her 6 more. Now she has 14 pennies. How many pennies did Sue start with? Have the child use counters to solve the problems.	for the first problem: _____ uses the counters to show 5 + 5. _____ identifies the answer as 10 apples. for the second problem: _____ uses the counters to show 14 − 6. _____ identifies the answer as 8 pennies.

terials: 10-frame, counters

TEST ITEM	EVALUATE WHETHER CHILD

26-A.1 *To add basic facts with sums 11 to 18 by making a ten and more*
 	
Give the child counters and a 10-frame, and write the following problems on cards or paper:
 	
    8   9
   + 3   + 5
 	
Have the child explain how to use counters and a 10-frame to find each sum and then solve each problem.
	_____ explains how to use the counters and the 10-frame to find each sum.
	
	_____ identifies the sums as 11 and 14.

26-A.2 *To add three numbers with sums from 11 to 18 by using* **doubles** *or* **making a ten**
 	
Write the following facts on cards or paper:
 	
    7   8
    5   8
   + 3   + 2
 	
Have the child explain how to make a ten or use doubles to find each sum and then solve.
	_____ explains a strategy that could be used to solve each problem; for example,
	
	$\left.\begin{array}{r}7\\5\\+3\end{array}\right\}$ → make a ten
	
	$\left.\begin{array}{r}8\\8\\+2\end{array}\right\}$ → doubles
	
	_____ identifies the sums as 15 and 18.

26-A.3 *To use inverse operations to find sums and differences to 18* Write the following pairs of facts on cards or paper: 7 13 9 17 + 6 − 6 + 8 − 9 Have the child explain how to find each sum or difference and then solve each problem.	_____ explains that the addition and subtraction problems in each pair have the same numbers. _____ identifies the answers as 13, 7, 17, and 8.

Evaluation of Interview/Task Test

Date _____

Child's Name _____

Materials: connecting cubes

TEST ITEM	EVALUATE WHETHER CHILD
27-A.1 *To make equal groups and count to show how many in all* Have the child use cubes to make 4 groups with 3 cubes in each group. Then have the child tell how many cubes in all.	_____ makes 4 groups with 3 cubes in each group. _____ identifies the number of cubes as 12.
27-A.2 *To divide a group of objects into equal groups to determine how many go in each group and how many groups there are* Have the child divide 8 cubes into 4 equal groups. Have the child tell how many cubes go in each group. Then have the child divide 10 cubes, putting 5 in each group. Have the child tell how many groups there are.	_____ makes 4 groups with 2 cubes in each. _____ identifies the number in each group as 2. _____ makes 2 groups with 5 cubes in each. _____ identifies the number of groups as 2.
27-A.3 *To solve problems by **drawing a picture*** Read the following story problems: There are 4 plates. There are 3 cookies on each plate. How many cookies are there in all? There are 6 balloons. There are 2 children. Each child gets the same number of balloons. How many balloons does each child get? Have the child draw pictures to solve the problems.	_____ draws an appropriate picture for the first problem. _____ identifies the number of cookies as 12. _____ draws an appropriate picture for the second problem. _____ identifies the number of balloons each child gets as 3.

terials: Workmat 3, base-ten blocks

TEST ITEM	EVALUATE WHETHER CHILD

28-A.1 *To add and subtract tens*
 	
Write the following problems on cards or paper:
 	
    20   60
  + 50   − 10
 	
Have the child explain how to use base-ten blocks with Workmat 3 to find the sum or difference.
	first problem:
	
	_____ explains that you put 2 tens in the tens column on the workmat and then put 5 more tens in the tens column. Then you add the tens.
	
	_____ identifies the sum as 70.
	
	second problem:
	
	_____ explains that you put 6 tens in the tens column on the workmat and then take away 1 ten.
	
	_____ identifies the difference as 50.

28-A.2 *To add and subtract tens and ones*
 	
Write the following problems on cards or paper:
 	
    32   57
  + 26   − 33
 	
Have the child explain how to use base-ten blocks with Workmat 3 to find the sum or difference.
	first problem:
	
	_____ explains that you put 3 tens in the tens column and 2 ones in the ones column on the workmat. Then you put 2 more tens in the tens column and 6 more ones in the ones column. Then you add, starting in the ones column.
	
	_____ identifies the sum as 58.
	
	second problem:
	
	_____ explains that you put 5 tens in the tens column and 7 ones in the ones column on the workmat. Then you take away 3 tens and 3 ones, starting in the ones column.
	
	_____ identifies the difference as 24.

28-A.3 *To choose a reasonable estimate to solve problems* Read the following story problem with the 3 answer choices: Beth has 38 pennies. She spends 17 pennies. How many pennies does she have left? 2 pennies 21 pennies 210 pennies Have the child choose the answer choice that makes sense for the problem and explain his or her choice.	_____ identifies 21 as the answer choice that makes sense. _____ explains that 21 makes sense because Beth had about 40 and took away about 20, which makes the answer about 20.

MATH ADVANTAGE
Grade 1

Performance Assessment

Class Record Form • Page 1

Teacher _____

112

1-A.1	To use concrete materials to model addition story problems	
1-A.2	To add on 1 or 2 to find sums to 6	
1-A.3	To use pictures to find sums	
1-A.4	To write and solve addition sentences to represent addition story problems	
2-A.1	To use concrete materials to model subtraction story problems	
2-A.2	To subtract 1 or 2 to find differences from 6	
2-A.3	To write and solve subtraction sentences to represent pictures	
2-A.4	To use the strategy *make a model* to solve addition and subtraction story problems	
3-A.1	To use counters to understand the Commutative Property of Addition	
3-A.2	To identify combinations of addends with sums to 10	
3-A.3	To add basic facts to 10 in vertical and horizontal formats	
3-A.4	To use the strategy *make a model* to solve addition problems with money	

Performance Assessment

Class Record Form • Page 2

Teacher _____

4-A.1	To use the *counting on* strategy to add	
4-A.2	To use counters to show doubles and write the facts	
4-A.3	To find sums for addition facts to 10	
4-A.4	To use the strategy *drawing a picture* to solve problems	
5-A.1	To identify combinations of ways to subtract from numbers 10 or less	
5-A.2	To subtract in horizontal and vertical formats	
5-A.3	To identify fact families with sums to 10	
5-A.4	To use subtraction to compare two groups of 10 or less	
6-A.1	To use the *counting back* strategy to subtract	
6-A.2	To subtract zero and subtract to find a difference of zero	
6-A.3	To find sums and differences for addition and subtraction facts to 10	
6-A.4	To use the strategy *drawing a picture* to solve problems	
7-A.1	To identify solid figures	
7-A.2	To sort solid figures by attributes	
7-A.3	To sort use the strategy *make a model* to identify how many cubes are used to build a figure	

Performance Assessment

Class Record Form • Page 3

Teacher _____

8-A.1	To identify plane figures																					
8-A.2	To sort plane figures by the number of sides and corners																					
8-A.3	To identify figures that have the same size and shape																					
8-A.4	To identify a line of symmetry in plane figures																					
9-A.1	To identify plane figures as open or closed																					
9-A.2	To classify objects by position																					
9-A.3	To locate positions on a grid																					
10-A.1	To identify, reproduce, and extend patterns																					
10-A.2	To create patterns																					
10-A.3	To analyze and correct patterns																					
11-A.1	To use strategies such as *counting on* and *doubles* to find sums to 12																					
11-A.2	To add three addends with sums through 12																					
11-A.3	To solve addition story problems by acting them out and writing addition sentences to represent the problems																					

Performance Assessment

Class Record Form • Page 4

Teacher _____

12-A.1	To use mental math strategies such as *counting back, relating addition and subtraction,* and *fact families* to find differences to 12
12-A.2	To compare groups of objects to find the differences between them
12-A.3	To solve addition and subtraction story problems by writing a number sentence
13-A.1	To count groups of tens, identify and write the number
13-A.2	To count groups of tens and ones to 100, identify and write the number
13-A.3	To use 10 as a benchmark to estimate a quantity as more than or fewer than 10
14-A.1	To identify ordinal numbers from *first* through *twelfth*
14-A.2	To compare two numbers and identify which number is greater or less
14-A.3	To identify numbers that come before, after, or between other numbers
14-A.4	To order numbers (less than 100) from least to greatest or from greatest to least
15-A.1	To count by twos, fives, and tens to 100
15-A.2	To identify a number as even or odd

Performance Assessment

Class Record Form • Page 5

Teacher _____

16-A.1	To count groups of pennies and groups of nickels and give the value
16-A.2	To count groups of dimes and give the value
16-A.3	To count combinations of nickels and pennies and give the value
16-A.4	To count combinations of dimes and pennies and give the value
16-A.5	To use the strategy make a model to identify coins they could use to buy an object
17-A.1	To trade pennies for nickels and dimes
17-A.2	To use combinations of coins to show a given amount using the fewest coins
17-A.3	To identify what coins are needed to purchase an item
17-A.4	To make combinations of pennies, nickels, and dimes that represent the value of a quarter
18-A.1	To read a calendar
18-A.2	To sequence events
18-A.3	To estimate which of two tasks will take more time
19-A.1	To tell time to the hour and half hour
19-A.2	To estimate the time needed to do a

Class Record Form • Page 6

20-A.1	To use nonstandard units to measure length																									
20-A.2	To measure the length of objects in inches																									
20-A.3	To measure the length of objects in centimeters																									
21-A.1	To estimate, then weigh, using a balance to determine which of two objects is heavier																									
21-A.2	To estimate, then weigh, using nonstandard objects																									
21-A.3	To estimate, then measure, about how many cups a container will hold																									
21-A.4	To classify the temperature of objects as hot or cold																									
22-A.1	To identify equal parts, halves, fourths, and thirds of a whole																									
22-A.2	To visualize results of sharing equal parts to solve problems																									
22-A.3	To identify equal parts of a group																									
23-A.1	To sort objects and record data in a tally table																									
23-A.2	To use data to determine if an outcome is certain or impossible, or which event is most likely																									
23-A.3	To make predictions and record data in tally tables																									

MATH ADVANTAGE
Grade 1

Performance Assessment

Class Record Form • Page 7

Teacher _____

24-A.1	To record and interpret data in picture graphs																											
24-A.2	To count, record, and interpret data in tally tables and bar graphs																											
25-A.1	To find sums to 18 using mental math strategies such as *doubles, doubles plus one,* and *doubles minus one*																											
25-A.2	To write the related addition and subtraction number sentences for doubles fact families																											
25-A.3	To solve story problems by modeling																											
26-A.1	To add basic facts with sums 11–18 by using *making a ten and more*																											
26-A.2	To add three numbers with sums 11–18 by using *doubles or making a ten strategy*																											
26-A.3	To use inverse operations to finds sums and differences to 18																											

118

Class Record Form • Page 8

Teacher _____

27-A.1	To make equal groups and count to show how many in all																								
27-A.2	To put objects into equal groups to determine how many in each group and how many groups																								
27-A.3	To solve problems by _drawing a picture_																								
28-A.1	To add and subtract tens																								
28-A.2	To add and subtract tens and ones																								
28-A.3	To choose a reasonable estimate to solve problems																								